NEW PLAINS REVIEW

SPRING 2019

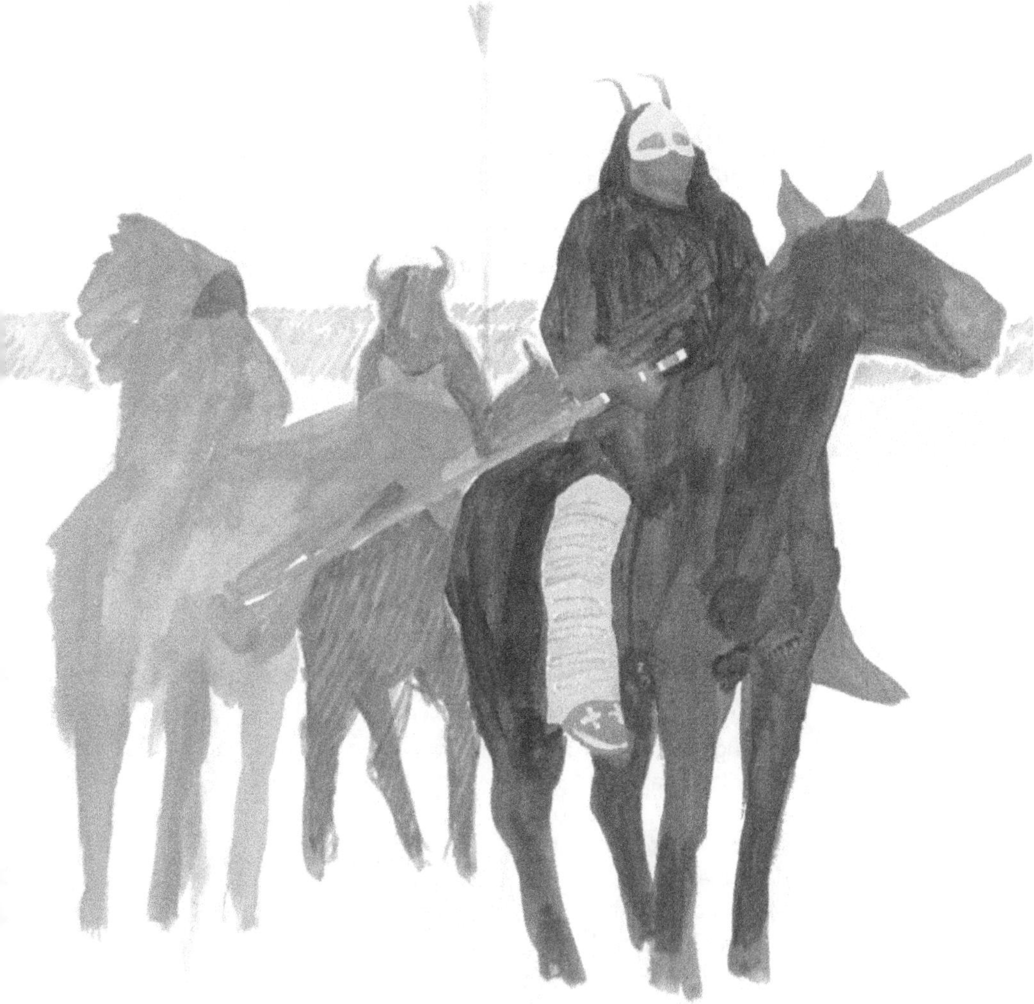

New Plains Student Publishing
University of Central Oklahoma
Edmond, Oklahoma

NEW PLAINS REVIEW

is edited by students and faculty of the English Department in the College of Liberal Arts at The University of Central Oklahoma. Political, social or artistic commentary represents the views of the writers and artists, and inclusion in the journal does not indicate editorial endorsement or non-endorsement. New Plains Review does not claim to represent the views of the University or its officials.

The image found on the previous page is from a painting titled *Phantom Warriors* by acclaimed Native American artist and UCO alumnus Sherman Chaddlesone.

Visit our website at *newplainsreview.com*
Email inquiries to *newplainsreview@gmail.com*

English Department, Box 184
University of Central Oklahoma
100 North University Drive
Edmond, Oklahoma 73034

Published in USA; printing & manufacturing information can be found on the final page.

ISBN-10: 0-9984061-5-5
ISBN-13: 978-0-9984061-5-2

Table of Contents

TABLE OF CONTENTS

Foreword

It IS WITH MUCH EXCITEMENT THAT WE welcome you to yet another edition of the *New Plains Review*. Since its inaugural issue in 1986, New Plains has grown to represent the creative works of local and international authors and artists alike. With this in mind, the staff would like to thank our contributors, with special thanks to artist Esteban Jimenez Guerra, who submitted the cover image, "Del Mar y sus Testigos". Each semester, we take on the daunting task of selecting key works of prose, poetry, plays, graphic shorts, and visual art, with the goal of creating a unique blend of voices across multiple forms.

As with every edition, we were blown away by the sheer variety of submissions we received for this journal. While previous issues of New Plains have focused on specific tones and styles, this particular edition seems to have developed a personality of its own, showcasing an array of subgenres and themes. We hope that this journal represents the diverse passions and interests of our contributors, staff, and readers.

In addition to the works in this journal, we also have a collection of online exclusives— such as videos, audio recordings, and full color art submissions—which can be found at newplainsreview.com.

On behalf of the English Department, College of Liberal Arts, University of Central Oklahoma, we are proud to present the Spring 2019 edition of *New Plains Review*.

Zoe Wright
Editor-in-Chief

PROSE

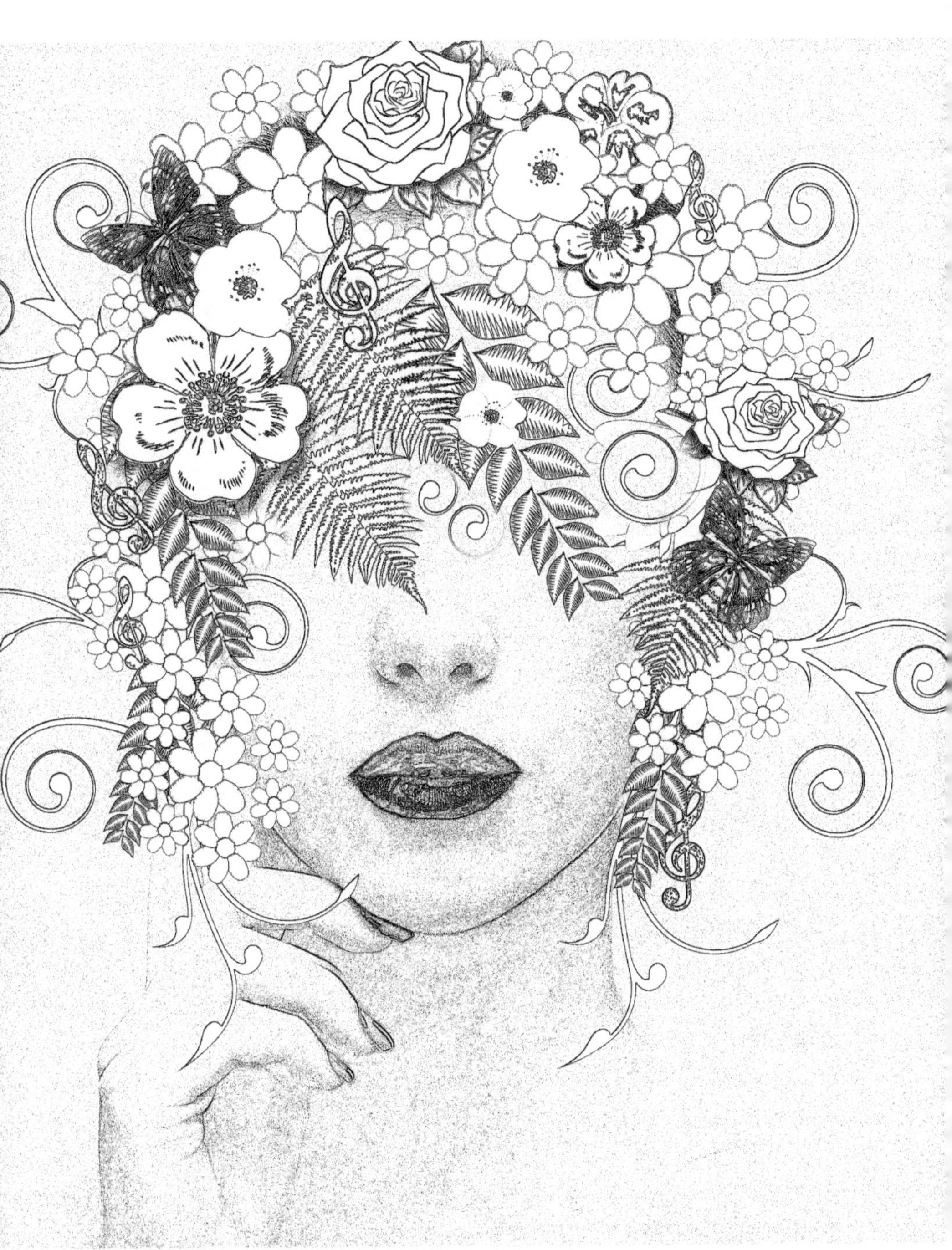

IMAGE BY SABINE SAUERMAUL (CREATIVECOMMONS.ORG)

Mr. Ratite's Avian Conservatory

BY EVAN JAMES SHELDON

Adam was breaking his mother's rules. He wandered a couple of blocks from Dana's Apartments with its crooked white, wooden sign, where he and his mother were currently staying. *Dana's* had been painted over *Moonlit*, but you could still see the outline underneath the new name. They were single-level stripmall-esque apartments. The kind where men whose wives were finally fed up with their shit stayed. The kind where the owner (presumably Dana) still offered an hourly rate. And the kind where a mother and son might stay if they didn't want to be found.

Adam was supposed to be staying in their room. For safety, his mother had said, and he had—for the first few days. He had to stay inside, and it would all be different. They would be staying longer this time, she said. It would be better, she said. She said many things. Adam wondered when he had stopped believing her.

It was sunny out and hot, but still chilly in the shade. On the cracked sidewalk, he jumped back and forth between the sun and the shade. Adam had never been to the ocean, but he imagined that he was hopping on a shoreline. He figured they were about as far from the ocean as they could get. This time, his mother had stopped somewhere in Colorado this time, and snow-capped mountains rose in the distance. The rocky peaks seemed to thrum with adventure. They called to him, whispering of magic, deep caves, and sheer cliffs. Adam turned around and walked away from them and toward a line of dingy stores.

He walked by the glass doors and neon signs, and debated stealing a book from the used bookstore. Or at least attempting to steal one. Store owners always seemed to be wary of thirteen-year-olds. Then he noticed a strange building off to the far end of the storefronts. A three-story house with a wraparound porch on the lower level stood all alone without other houses in the plots next to it. Fungus-gray paint was chipping, and various evergreen trees and unkempt bushes threatened to overtake the property. The house had two large white pillars in the front and looked like it was leaning on them, like an old person might lean on one of those walkers with the cut tennis balls on the feet.

A huge cage made from chain-link fence butted up next to the house. The top reached just above the windows on the first floor, and it was at least twenty feet wide going to the side and the back. A man in a wheelchair swung an old straw broom at something that hung down from the top of the cage. There were a bunch of hanging things.

Birds. The old man was swatting at birds. Stuffed birds with their wings flung out wide, talons splayed, swaying on wires so thin that Adam could barely see them. The old man was whacking away at a bird that looked like a miniature eagle. As he hit the bird, it swung out wide, and the snow on its back slid off and landing on the man's lap. He made such a startled, scrunched-up, bulgy-eyed face that Adam laughed.

The man's skin was the color of a wooden fence in need of stain and, if his nose was any indication, he had been in more than one fistfight. Barely visible wisps of white hair drifted around his ears like clean smoke. He grumbled something under his breath and made his way to the next the bird.

"What are you doing in there? Why do you have all those birds?" Adam called.

The man didn't bother to look over at Adam and just shouted, "Closed!" He went back to hitting the birds with his broom.

It was kind of sad to watch the old man stretch and swing at the birds, trying to knock the snow off them. Most he could barely reach, even with the broom. Sometimes he would miss and swear, never taking his eyes off his target. Adam was standing only a few feet away, but he might as well have been a ghost for all the attention he was getting. More than feeling bad for the old guy, Adam wanted more snow to fall on him. Maybe on his head this time. Cool him off a bit.

After a few minutes and no snow-to-old-guy-face, Adam went to the front door. Locked. To the right of the door stood a dirty plaque. Adam pulled his sweatshirt sleeve down over his hand to brush the dirt and snow from its brass face.

MR. RATITE'S AVIAN CONSERVATORY

HRS. VARY

∞

Adam made it back to Dana's Apartments before his mother. He kicked off his shoes and laid on the thin, papery mattress, trying to find something good on T.V. He ended up choosing an old Western. The kind where you could immediately tell who the bad guy was by the curve of his moustache and foreboding music. It was nice not to be confused about who the bad guy was.

He rummaged around the apartment, which was really more like a shitty motel. He found a pocket-sized lime green Bible, a black ballpoint pen, and some tiny sticky notes. Taking all three, he stuffed them under his side of the mattress with his other collectables. A couple marbles from that place in Santa Fe. A small stack of nudie pics that he'd found littering the street corners in Las Vegas. *Stranger in a Strange Land*, which he had reread so many times while they were driving, that the gummy binding was exposed and cracking. His father's watch. He didn't have any plans for the stuff. Sometimes he just took things. Everything was where it needed to be when his mother opened the door. Her jaw was clenched and her eyes red. She liked to lick her lips when she was nervous, and Adam could see that the skin around her mouth was chapped and irritated. Her arms wrapped around her purse like a child might clutch a teddy bear—she was smiling.

"How did it go?" Adam asked, turning down the television.

"Okay." She sniffed. "Okay I think. They said that they'll call here when they make a decision."

Adam knew just as well as she did that no one ever called. Not for the kind of job she was looking for: waitress, bagger, checkout girl. Any sort of job that preferred a pretty smile over a clean background check.

"That's good, at least," Adam's tone sounded hollow even to him. Sometimes it was hard to fake hopeful.

But it seemed to have helped, and his mother's eyes lit up just a bit, the ghost of a real smile threatening to emerge. "Right? Maybe they'll call. Will you answer if I'm out?"

Adam nodded.

"Tomorrow is a new day. This place is going to be different. I just know it. How was it here today?"

He shrugged and turned the Western up. "Pretty good. Just watched some shows. You know. Lounged."

If she didn't believe him, she didn't say it. She walked

by on the way to the bathroom and squeezed one of his socked
feet.

Later, when she got into bed smelling of cheap soap and
shampoo, and cheaper booze, Adam didn't say anything either,
pretending to be asleep. He knew the shooter bottles would be
gone by the time he got up. It was an agreement of sorts. She
snuggled over next to him and he wondered if someone could get
drunk on the heady aroma of peppermint schnapps.

The next day, he went back to Mr. Ratite's Avian
Conservatory. There was something about it that intrigued him.
Maybe because it was just so weird. Maybe because there wasn't
really any other place to go.

The front door was unlocked. Adam didn't wait for an
invitation. The whole place was filled with stuffed birds: vulture-
esque ones, both small and large, with bald heads; beautiful, tiny
birds with colors that made peacocks seem drab; an ostrich that
was taller than Adam on his tiptoes reared in the corner. Sleek
birds, ruffled birds, green birds, blue birds, ones that looked like
something out of a horror movie, and ones so cute and tiny that
Adam wanted to pick them up and rub them against his face.
Each bird had a tiny wooden plaque next to it that listed what
he assumed was its scientific name and a tiny spotlight shining
on the birds up from below. Some of the bulbs were out, giving
Adam the impression that the birds were hiding in the dark.
Maybe some others perched out of sight, waiting. It was creepy,
but kind of awesome at the same time.

The walls and floors of the house were all old, wooden,
and in need of dusting. It smelled musty and like burnt cookies.
To the right, there was a staircase equipped with one of those
automated chairs that rode up and down on a track along the wall.
On the left, stood a bookshelf with a tacky, handwritten sign that
read: ALL BOOKS $5. Adam scanned them briefly—they were all
about birds. He grabbed one at random and put it inside his jacket.

Adam found Mr. Ratite in a back room. The old man
didn't turn at first, and Adam tried to be quiet, to watch for a
moment. He couldn't tell how tall the man was since he was
sitting in his wheelchair, but Adam guessed that, even hunched
over like that, the man used to be imposing. Mr. Ratite was
focused on a bar cart in front of him and poured some liquid that

looked like a mixture of piss and syrup into fake-frosted glasses. The old man turned. Adam froze, not sure what he should do, but Mr. Ratite didn't say anything or look surprised. He was wearing a seatbelt across his lap. Wiggling both glasses between his too-thin legs, he rolled over next to Adam. He passed a glass to Adam, who had no intention of drinking it.

Mr. Ratite made his way over to a sliding glass door that led outside. He pushed it open and rolled down the ramp into the cage with the hanging birds. One of his wheelchair tires needed lubrication and it made a rasping squawk whenever he turned on it. Adam followed him outside.

Mr. Ratite snatched up the same broom as the day before, but this time he was sweeping up fallen feathers off the concrete.

"What's your name, kid?" He didn't turn away from his task.

"Adam."

"Okay, Adam. Do you know how a bird is able to fly?"

Adam thought it was probably speed, or lift versus weight, or something scientific like that, but he'd also been around enough to recognize a setup, so he didn't respond.

Mr. Ratite pushed more feathers into wet piles. "No guesses? Don't want to embarrass yourself in front of our noble friends here?" The way he said noble made Adam think the word somehow wasn't enough.

"They are torn between the heavens and the earth. Something pulls them up, and something pulls them down. They aren't really home at home in the middle, but it is the best they can do," Mr. Ratite said. When Adam didn't respond, Mr. Ratite said, "Or maybe it's just invisible strings."

Adam laughed, surprised.

"That must be it. Invisible strings that pull them up." Mr. Ratite used the broom to poke at a bird that looked like a hawk. The bird had been posed with its talons wide and hooked beak slightly open. As it careened about from the shove, Adam could almost believe it was swooping in for an attack. Almost real.

"If they're held up by strings," Adam asked, "what are the strings attached to? What moves them around?"

Mr. Ratite stopped poking at the bird and seemed to really look at Adam for the first time. "Isn't it obvious?"

When Adam didn't say anything, Mr. Ratite laughed. It wasn't a mean laugh, though, and Adam chuckled at the joke even though he didn't understand. Sometimes it was better to just go along. Their shared laughter died quickly, as a pained look crossed Mr. Ratite's face, and he rolled inside. It looked difficult, but when Adam moved to help, Mr. Ratite waved him off. He was breathing heavily, and droplets of sweat began to form on his forehead. His coffee-colored face looked like someone had stirred in too much cream. Adam set his cup down on an end table and moved in to help, though he had no idea what he was going to do.

"Leave. Please." Mr. Ratite's speech was slurred a bit, and he swung a long arm at Adam. It was a slow swing, but Adam scooted back and knocked over his glass. It shattered on the floor. The acidic-sweet smell of lemonade floated up around him. Adam bolted to the front door and looked back. Mr. Ratite shook violently and his chair bounced with his movements. Adam ran, not bothering to shut the door behind him.

"Do you ever miss it? Home?"

Adam's mother had gotten a job at a Safeway earlier and had celebrated by buying a pint of cinnamon whiskey. They were lying on the bed and playing UNO. Some of the cards were missing, but it didn't change the game. She occasionally walked to the window to blow cigarette smoke out through the screen. Adam sneaked a pull off the bottle when she wasn't looking. It burned like cider that had gone horribly wrong and made everything feel softer around his eyes. His mother only drank whiskey to celebrate, but it also made her nostalgic.

"No. I mean there's things I miss, maybe," he said. "Like playing baseball or going to the library. But altogether I don't miss it. You?"

He played a green Draw Two. They never mentioned him when they talked about home. It was part of their agreement. She swore under her breath, perhaps at whatever cards she had drawn.

"Of course not. Well, maybe a couple things. My garden. Do you remember how good those beefsteak tomatoes were?"

Adam secretly hated tomatoes, but he had pretended to like them to make her smile. He didn't say anything and played a red Reverse.

"But most of it I'm glad to be without. This is so much better."

Adam looked around, and it was probably the whiskey, but for what seemed like the first time in a long time, he agreed with his mother. She played a Wild Draw Four, and he didn't even curse.

☙

The next time Adam walked over to the Conservatory, he wondered what he was doing. Did he want to go because he felt bad for leaving like he had? Guilty for stealing the book and not helping Mr. Ratite? The place was really kind of gross. But there was something about it, the weird birds and Mr. Ratite himself, that made him want to go back. The old guy was clearly crazy, but kind of funny, and Adam didn't know anyone else.

Adam walked in and Mr. Ratite acted like nothing had happened. No seizure, no broken glass, no stolen book. If anything, it made Mr. Ratite easier to be around. Not talking about something awkward, even horrible, was a specialty for Adam.

This time Mr. Ratite had put out some terrible lemon cookies hardened like jawbreakers. Adam snapped them into pieces on a tiny plate and sucked on the shards while Mr. Ratite showed him around the Conservatory. Most of what he said was interesting, but there was only so much scientific jargon one person can hear about birds before they start to zone out. He was going on and on about some bird named *Gyps Fulvus*, but all Adam could think of was that the name sounded like a part of the female anatomy he'd just recently become interested in.

"*Gyps Fulvus* is a stupid name," Adam blurted. He halfway expected Mr. Ratite to get mad, like most adults when Adam interrupted. But Mr. Ratite just wheezed and chuckled.

"Of course. Of course. Adam. I should have guessed. A man made of the earth, born of the sky! A divinely give name." By the end he was almost yelling and made some grand flourish with his hands. Adam was sure he was being mocked, but it didn't feel mean-spirited. Plus, he had just been called a man. At least someone noticed.

"What would you call this creature, Adam?"

"I don't know. What does it do?"

Mr. Ratite raised an eyebrow. "So perhaps a bit of wisdom after all. It's a vulture. It scavenges. It steals. It hisses while it eats and roosts."

Adam thought for a moment. "How about Gross-Necked Thiever? It doesn't include the hissing, but at least it's better than

Gyps Fulvus."

"Perhaps it is. Perhaps it is. I think, young Adam, that it might be best if you take your leave."

He worried he had upset Mr. Ratite, but saw that same draining look on the old man's face, and his dark hands gripped the wheels of his chair tight enough that Adam thought the twisting veins there might rupture. Adam set the plate down, now filled with lemon flavored dust and splinters. He ran back to Dana's Apartments, the whole time wondering how long Mr. Ratite's chair would shake and rattle.

Adam began sneaking out every day to visit the Conservatory. Soon, slush and snow gave way to warm showers and cool evenings. They sucked on rock-hard cookies and drank the thick lemonade that Adam quickly came to love. They talked about shapes of feathers, mating habits, migratory patterns, and anything bird-related. There were things they didn't talk about too. Like that Adam had discovered that Mr. Ratite was not a real name. Like the photo of a younger Mr. Ratite, standing and holding hands with a smiling woman. They never spoke about their pasts, as if they both knew that topic was best left alone, though Adam gathered Mr. Ratite used to be in the military. Adam oiled Mr. Ratite's wheel when it got squeaky.

One day Adam came home, finding his mother sitting cross-legged on the bed with roadmaps surrounding her. She had a blue sharpie out and the cap stuck in her mouth. Thin blue lines curled and waggled across the different maps, tracing different routes, different possibilities. The room smelled of peppermint.

Without speaking, Adam gently began to scoop up the maps. He folded them slowly, so she could see he was being careful with her plans. He climbed on the bed and pulled the cap from her mouth, placing it back on the sharpie. By the time he had finished, she was crying.

"Just for a while longer," Adam said.

His mother had covered her face when she began to cry. Now she took her shaking hands away and he saw her eyes were wide and wild, like a frightened animal about to run. But she didn't run. She slowly nodded, and then Adam hugged her.

The next week, his mother got him enrolled in a local middle school. He couldn't go over to Mr. Ratite's quite as often. Once, a group of kids at school heard him talking about the Conservatory and tee peed the cage with the dangling birds. Adam climbed up the fence and tore it all down. The next time he went in the conservatory, he saw a handwritten sign that read *Gross-Necked Thiever* had been taped over the old *Gyps Fulvus* plaque. After that, he didn't talk about the Conservatory at school.

His mother got him a library card. They would sit up in bed reading novels in the morning. At night, his mother drank cinnamon whiskey more and more often than peppermint schnapps. When she fell asleep, he would pull out the book he had stolen. And, using the tiny stick-it notes, he renamed the birds. "*Spilornis Klossiwith*, common green snake," became "Newsboy Dragon Slayer." "*Micastur Mirandollei*," who had a seven-to-ten-note vocal range and liked to eat rats, became the "Pied Piper Falcon." It wasn't long and the whole book teemed with little yellow notes.

The week before summer break, Adam decided to skip class after lunch. No one would miss him in study hall. Mr. Hathaway watched videos on Facebook with his headphones on the whole time and didn't even bother with attendance. No one noticed as Adam left school and made his way to Mr. Ratite's. He had stolen a cigarette from his mother's pack and smoked it as he walked.

When he arrived, he found Mr. Ratite up front trimming the plants that threatened to overtake his porch. He dropped the shears and greeted Adam with a smile.

"Playing hooky? I never liked school either. Until I got to the university. That's when it gets good." He looked healthier and his dark skin glistened warmly. "Want to go inside? I just finished baking some cookies."

Adam tried not to grimace. "No thanks." He had planned this to be a grand gesture. A way of saying thank you. A way of saying, "you're weird, but I am too, and that's cool." A way of saying something he couldn't vocalize. But now that he was here, he felt awkward. "Here," he said, and pushed the stolen book into Mr. Ratite's hands.

"I knew you would bring it back. I knew it." Mr. Ratite opened the book and read some of the sticky notes. If his skin had been glistening before, it was nothing compared to his eyes now. "I have most of these in the Conservatory. Let's go change the names! Adam?"

But Adam wasn't listening to Mr. Ratite anymore. He could only watch as his mother pulled up, the sedan's brakes squealing as she slammed to a stop half on, half off the curb. She frantically waved for him to join her, but he didn't. He just stood there, wanting to run, yet somehow unable. Like she had a gravity about her, and now that she was this near, there was no escape.

She hopped out and didn't bother to shut the driver's side door. "You weren't at school. I thought he had gotten you."

"I just come over here sometimes and help out. This is Mr. Ratite."

His mother grabbed his upper arm. She was fast. He had forgotten how fast she could be. "You think I don't know that? You think I didn't know that you come here?"

Adam tried to shrug out of her grip, but he couldn't. "You followed me?"

"Of course, I followed you. I've always followed you."

Something in Adam deflated with that. Something lost ground, lost wind. "Where do you think you saw him?" he asked.

"Think I saw him? White F150. Thin-rimmed glasses. Wide brimmed hat. Shirt unbuttoned and slack. That scar on his neck. It was him. You think I wouldn't recognize your father?"

She pulled on him, but Adam didn't want to move. He kept his footing and fought against her. He was not as small as he used to be.

"Henry! Get in the car now!" She was nearly screaming by the end of the sentence.

Mr. Ratite spoke up and startled them both.

"I don't know who you are, Ma'am, but I think you are confused. This is Adam and we were just about to head inside for some cookies so…"

"Oh, God. His name's not Adam. It's Henry. He's been lying to you. Last time I think it was Michael. The next spot it will be something different." Adam pulled away from her and took a step away. He didn't run though. He was tired of running. A nasty look spread across his mother's face as she addressed Mr. Ratite. "You don't know him. Just because you spend a little time together, you think you know him? No. He's mine. He's always been mine."

She locked eyes with Henry. "And now we have to go. He's coming."

Henry looked back and forth between the two, and then said something he'd only ever thought. When he said it, he spoke quietly, like, if he were gentle with the words, their truth might escape out into the world, without crumbling beneath their own weight. "He's not coming for us. He was never coming for us."

His mother let out a sound that was something between a sob and wail. It came out low and dirty. It was horrible for him to hear. Because he knew then that no matter what he said in the future, he couldn't take it back, and no matter what happened in the future, she wouldn't believe him. Something had broken between them.

He thought she might crumple then, just fall and lie still, but she rose straighter than ever.

"Get in the car. Now."

"I'm not going. I'm—"

He reached for Mr. Ratite and snagged the arm of his chair, and his mother lunged. She wrapped both arms around his waist. For a moment, Henry hung between the two while Mr. Ratite tried to hold on to Henry's hands.

But his mother yanked. The seatbelt kept Mr. Ratite from being pulled out of his chair, but the book was jostled from his lap and fell, hitting the sidewalk and springing open. Henry kept scrabbling for Mr. Ratite's hand, but he found no purchase. She set him in the car like a child.

She drove away blotchy-faced and silent. She didn't even bother to light up a cigarette. Henry briefly considered taking one out and lighting it up, but he couldn't. He wouldn't. At least not right now. There would be plenty of time for that at the next stop. His mother was crying still, but her jaw was set. The floorboard beneath his feet had his book, his marbles, and even his father's watch. All the things he had thought hidden from her, except for the nudie pics. He picked up his things and thought he would need to steal his mother some Chapstick at the next gas station. Her lips always did get so chapped when she was stressed.

Henry glanced in the rearview mirror and watched as Mr. Ratite struggled to pick up the tiny yellow sticky notes that had fluttered to the ground around him like fallen feathers.

Skyway

BY KATE SPITZMILLER

The same night Andre Dubus III told me he loved my work and high-fived me over a garbage can outside Miller Auditorium, someone jumped from the Skyway Bridge.

"People do it all the time," my cabbie said. "It's 'cause it almost always works."

Flashing blue and red lights swirled past us on the overpass.

"They don't even make the news anymore," he said.

A suicide. Around thirty minutes after I'd received the compliment of my life from a *New York Times* Bestselling Author. Coincidence, I wondered? Or a message?

My first real attempt was in March of 2003. I went for the double whammy: pills and carbon monoxide. When the bottle of Ativan didn't seem to be working, I went down to the garage of my townhouse, turned on the car, sat down against the rear tire, and breathed.

I gave up after a time. I don't know why. There was no great flash of regret, no sudden realization that I wanted to live. I just gave up on giving up. I called my doctor of five years and she called an ambulance. The ambulance never showed up, so I drove myself to the ER.

I forced down a paper cup of liquid charcoal so they wouldn't have to pump my stomach. I marveled that the deputy sheriff hanging around beside my bed was actually there for me. I couldn't decide whether he was protecting everyone else from me or protecting me from myself.

For three days, I was in the psych ward. Nothing much happened. I remember red Jell-O in little accordion paper cups and pea-green tiles in the shower and the scratchy orange couches in the common area. The TV was tuned perpetually to CNN. The United States was bombing the shit out of Iraq, and I suppose the patients in the psych ward needed to see it, too.

We were given the option of the nicotine patch or two cigarette breaks a day. Most of us chose the cigarette breaks. It was a chance to go outside, into some of those earliest days of spring, when you can smell the earth thawing and imagine the pale green shoots of the daffodils poking up through the piles of dirty grey snow. It was a chance to get a real hit of nicotine—straight to the bloodstream, straight to the brain. Cigarettes became my reason for living.

I'd called a few people from the little alcove where the payphone was and lied to most of them. Only my mom and my best friend, Sally, knew the truth. Sal was skittering about over in the UK, making arrangements to come across the Atlantic and get me out. She was a teacher and it was hard to get time off.

On the day Sal was due to arrive, I promised a grave-looking doctor with a forgettable name that I wouldn't try to hurt myself again. He made me write up a plan for the next time I felt suicidal, gave it a once-over, and then signed the necessary paperwork. All I wanted was a cigarette.

Sal arrived with a carton of duty-free Marlboro Lights. They released me into her custody and we went back to my townhouse. She stayed for a few days, made me laugh, helped me clean, and reminded me of the old days. We also planned ahead: a trip in April to the Turks and Caicos Islands to sleep on a friend's floor. Paradise on the cheap. Something to look forward to.

And here I was in paradise again. Saint Petersburg, Florida, sixteen years later. A cool January evening with my mind full of confidence, a sense of purpose because I had been praised by a writer I greatly admired. Yet, someone—I didn't know who—would never get that feeling. Had perhaps *never* had that feeling. And they had, that night, chosen to jump from a two-hundred-foot bridge into the dark cold of Tampa Bay.

And my cabbie was right, this person didn't make the news. I looked. I hit Google as soon as I arrived back at home in Massachusetts. I typed in "Skyway Bridge, Saint Petersburg, Florida, suicide, January 26, 2019." In return, I was given the "Skyway Bridge Jumper Report." Suicides are so common on the bridge that there is a website dedicated to them.

I survived my suicide attempt. And one more attempt in 2012. I lived long enough to hear Andre Dubus III yell out "I love your work!" and high-five me over a garbage can. I've had a novel published. And short stories.

But will I ever be free of it? Fixed? Will Winston Churchill's black dog ever truly leave my side? I have strange brain chemistry. Maybe the person on the Skyway Bridge did, too.

You see, the person who jumped from the Skyway Bridge is a shade of me. The way a shadow shows the shape of a thing, but darkly. We are the same, but one drawn more clearly than the other, one more present in the world. But the shadow me, she knows why the jumpers jump. She knows why the cold dark of the bay beckons more than the brightly-lit warmth of home. There are not words for this. It is enough to say that if you have been that shadow form, been that shade, you feel it strongly in others. You understand. You see the flashing blue and red lights swirl past you on the overpass and recognize the woman on the other side. She is you.

So, I think now that Andre Dubus III loved my work on that night for a reason. Shadows disappear when light is shone brightly upon them. Shade evaporates in the hot glow of the noonday sun.

The next time, I will stand in the light and not give in to the shadows. I will remember flashing blue and red lights swirling past and resist the dark cold of the bay.

I will remember a high-five given over a garbage can.

Extinct in the Wild

BY P.S. BECKET

"Quit tapping the glass, dear."

"Can we take it home, Mommy?"

"No, sweetie. It's against the rules."

"But Mommy!"

"No buts! Come on, the zoo is closing now."

"Yes, Mommy." The little girl backed away from the glass, leaving a faint circle of fog on it. After the two left the mammal exhibit, the overhead lights went out, leaving only the purple lights in the cages to illuminate the building. The last worker made his patrol around the exhibit before heading home for some much-needed rest. He took his time admiring the animals, taking in their natural beauty. He always reminded himself that he was lucky to see such creatures, as many of them were the last of their kind.

He stopped at his last and favorite creature, taking a moment to read the colorful plaque like he always did. The history of the odd-looking being fascinated him greatly, there was so much they didn't know about it. The plaque only offered vague details on the origin of the species, along with the only concrete fact they knew about it in red letters: MASS EXTINCTION: EXTINCT IN THE WILD. He felt sad for the little guy, he looked so scared, so alone.

"At least you're safe here." The worker grinned at the creature. It seemed to react to his voice, turning its head to him, showing him its big eyes. "See you tomorrow, buddy." The guard turned and walked out of the mammal exhibit, locking the doors behind him.

The purple lights in its cage gave off a continuous low hum, illuminating the rope swing that served as a bed in the corner, and the red ball under it. Food dishes were pressed against the glass so viewers could see it if it was hungry or thirsty. The three walls were covered in a beautiful picture of a tree in a meadow, with a beach far in the distance. In the wash of the eerie purple light it looked dreamlike, almost nightmarish. Bleeding out of the thick glass before it, the light illuminated the name of the species on the colorful plaque in a sickly violet: HUMAN.

The creature crawled into the rope swing, staring blankly at the bare ceiling. The familiar hum of the light above marching on through the night.

It was safe.

Snow-Drop

BY P.S. BECKET

The door hissed open and the figure stepped through. He was struggling to hit the big red button for the door from under three layers of coats, scarves, and snow. When he finally succeeded, the door slid shut behind him with a low hiss that gradually got higher before closing. He shrugged off the first layer and let it fall to the floor with a wet plop before removing his face mask. The welcome feeling of warm air hit his face and he breathed a sigh of relief; he was home.

Walking over to the terminal on the far wall of the airlock he typed in his code, relishing the responsive click of each key. The smaller door in front of him raised open and he stepped through while removing his second layer. He threw the wet coat on the lone bench to his right without looking and began to remove the smaller effects from his person. The gloves went first and joined the coat on the bench along with the scarf, heat pods, boots, two layers of socks, and the last over shirt. He slumped over to his favorite overstuffed chair and melted into it.

Before he could so much as take a breath, the screen in front of him jumped to life and the monotone voice of the base's AI began spouting off information.

OUTSIDE TEMPERATURE: NEGATIVE FORTY-FIVE DEGREES CELSIUS.

INTERIOR TEMPERATURE: TWENTY DEGREES CELSIUS.

SENSORS READ—

"Emergency override, code: 66789." The screen blinked off. He pressed the usual combination of buttons on the desk and a steaming mug shot up from the hole next to the screen. Grasping it, it took a minute for the warmth to spread through his hands before taking a sip. He leaned back, mug in hand, and took in his surroundings.

The base was small, but bigger than other ones he'd seen in pictures. The stone walls were lined with heat strips that glowed a bright orange; he often stared at the heat waves coming

off them when he was bored, which was frequently. The strips
also acted as light sources around the edges of the room, shining
amber light on the spots the huge overhead bulb missed from its
fixture in the center of the ceiling. Old robot arms and work tables
made up the clutter scattered across the room, along with other
stuff he found out in the wild. A few odd-colored rocks, some
tarnished remains of drones, anything he thought he could use.

He glanced at the digital clock on the wall: 14:00. Time
for the best part of his day. He leaned over and maneuvered a
metal arm with a microphone at the end, pointing it at his mouth.
He then hit the big green button on the little black box next to the
screen and was welcomed by the sound of static.

"This is Research Base 73-A on channel one. The date is
January thirteenth, 3187. I'll be rewinding the distress beacon on
this and every channel I can from fourteen hundred to twenty-one
hundred, when the Beta Satellite is in range. Please head to these
coordinates if you receive this message…" He pressed a few more
buttons and heard the familiar beacon start up. He then proceeded
to repeat the message on all eleven channels he had in range. After
that, he returned to channel one, and his real fun began.

"Alright, welcome back to 'Snow-Drop,' your savior
from insanity! I'm your host, Mathew Liam Jagger, from
Research Base 73-A: the home of rock and roll!" Jagger picked
up a small cartridge from his desk and pushed it into a slot in the
black box. "This one goes out to the unlucky guy or gal who hears
it! Remember, I send out my location every day from fourteen
hundred to twenty-one hundred. Stay frosty!"

Jagger leaned back in his chair again, sipping from
his mug and taking in the fast guitar riffs dancing on the radio
waves. He stared at the ceiling, but he didn't see it. He didn't feel
anything but the occasional warm liquid down his throat—and
that was it. All he did was listen. Listen, and wonder if anyone
else was listening too.

Southern Trees

BY MORGAN SMITH

Trees can bear scars too. Dark, puckered with sap and pitch—botched attempts by an axe or the vaguely violent will of a summer thunderstorm. These trees have borne witness to our worst moments, here beneath the sweltering sky, among the blackberry-laden bushes. Every slurred word that dripped from our lips coats their leaves like nectar, a sickly sweet scent rotting amongst their roots. They know our secrets, and they know our lies.

∽

"Coralee!"

"Yes, Mama?" Mama's voice is a flash of lightning. You always know the thunder is coming.

"Did you feed them chickens? And did you give 'em enough water? You know how they git in the summer." Mama doesn't talk the way that our neighbors to the south do, not a full drawl, just the touch of an accent to the tip of her tongue, turning get into git.

"I brought out three buckets this morning, Mama."

"Check 'em again in the afternoon. That may not be enough."

I want to roll my eyes, but I know she would likely roll up her newspaper and give me a good swat, the way she does with the chubby flies that feed on our table scraps. Besides, I know she's right. Virginia summers are brutal, the kind that leave your skin sweating like cold grapes at a picnic, making the little baby hairs stick to your cheeks and your face flush like someone caught you spying on that girl down the lane.

I hitch my skirt up around my knees. Mama says it's not ladylike, but I'm aiming to head down to the pond. She must hear the rustle from the next room over—the next thing I know her voice is ringing out again, muffled by the sleepy heat of the old farmhouse.

"Coralee?"

"Yes, Mama?"

"Where are you gettin' off to?"

"Just down to the crick, Mama. It's too dang hot to be stuck in the house."

"You finished your chores?"

"Yes, Mama."

"And where are the boys?"

"They're at Bobby Rider's house, just down the street a ways."

"Okay. Be back in time for lunch, you hear?"

"Yes, Mama."

And with the creak of springs and the racket of a screen door, I'm out. The field looks hot as anything this time of day, wheat-baked breeze ruffling the rolling golden grasses; but just past it lies the edge of the woods, where the burbling creek meets a cool pond. The hay tickles my ankles and swishes against my skirt on the way down, little seeds clinging in Rorschach patterns that would mean something if I only looked close enough.

The field would be cheery, if it weren't for the whispers.

Old places like to talk about what came before, what they've seen. I don't live in the Deep South: I'm closer to D.C. than Charlottesville, and we have more Targets than Walmarts, but still, there are some things you can't forget. Our farm has stood since 1792. I know what that means, even if my family doesn't.

The air changes when I step into the woods; still muggy, but now with a hint of Appalachian meltwater in the breeze. The pond glitters, dug out by calloused hands dark with dirt so many years ago. I slip out of my clothes, leaving a heap of sweat-stained cotton at the bank, and dive in. The water is silky on my skin, reeds tickling my back, minnows nibbling at my toes and fingers. Sometimes a current will brush up against me, the jetstream of some bigger animal swimming beneath me. I'm not scared though. I know this place. I know what has been here, and I know that trout aren't the thing that should horrify me. That—that is a secret held in banned history books and dark bands around branches.

I float, gazing up at the sky above me. Blue and blue for miles, the same sky that was here in 2001, in 1941, in 1929, in 1914, in 1860. The sky has watched this land through it all, from gunshots that rang out every fifteen seconds to fifteen gunshots in a second. It knows the taste of smoke from chestnuts, from gunpowder, from wood piles, and from funeral pyres.

I float under the branches of a poplar tree, old—older than most of the trees in the forest. I climbed this tree when I was little, scrambling up the branches one by one, scraped palms leaving spots of blood on the leaves. They drank it, hungry for the food they grew up on. Towards the top the air was thinner, older.

I scrambled out across the limb marveling at how straight it was, like the cross up at the altar. Marks marred the bark, ridges and grooves like the ones left behind when we untie the horses. I ran my finger along them, forgetting for a moment that I was nearer to sky than ground, that old three-groove bullets were still lodged here from the Civil War, that branches weren't made to bear the weight of humans.

Before long, I was in a hospital bed, stitches already promising a puckered scar along my forearm. In the pond water, the scar looks green, ghostlike, a whisper of the past.

I imagine falling now—bruised arms, scars, broken bones. I imagine the ones that didn't fall—bruised necks, closed throats, crushed hyoids.

Trees can bear scars too.

Sankapul

BY RONY KAMPALATH

I'll admit the comments began to rankle after a while. Made in jest as they were, by friends and family that meant no harm, I still became prickly in response to the endless refrain. My newborn daughter, it was said, looked nothing like me.

A number of amusing explanations were offered. Perhaps she was the cable guy's kid? Or maybe my genes were just weak and submissive? Maybe my wife, Anna, had cloned herself, and hadn't needed my help at all? *Yes, yes,* I nodded, trying to keep things light, *all of these were equally plausible.* But make no mistake, whether I showed my displeasure or not, these were all implicit attacks on my manhood. Or at least on my DNA. Maybe sensing something, my Korean mother-in-law whispered in my ear.

"Don't listen to them. She has your eyes."

"Really?" I asked, cocking my head and raising the sleeping baby in the crook of my arm to look at her face. I decided that she didn't have my eyes. My mother-in-law was seeing something that wasn't there. Anna's family members who couldn't see the baby in person called in on FaceTime.

"Oh my gosh, Anna! She's got perfect *sankapul!*"

Or alternatively,

"She looks exactly like you, but with perfect little *sankapul!*"

I can figure out the meaning of a lot of Korean words, but contextual clues weren't helping here. *Sankapul.* I happened to think that everything was perfect on my baby girl's tiny face, and couldn't isolate the thing her family was talking about. Finally, I gave in and asked my wife.

I can figure out the meaning of a lot of Korean words, but contextual clues weren't helping here. *Sankapul.* I happened to think that everything was perfect on my baby girl's tiny face, and couldn't isolate the thing her family was talking about. Finally, I gave in and asked my wife.

"It's the fold above your eyelid," she told me. "You have it. White people have it. But Asians don't."

I went to the bathroom to look at my face. Sure enough, when my eyes opened, the thin skin of my eyelid retracted into a fold under my brow which ran transversely across the length of my eye. I had never noticed this before, and I stared at it with the interest you might expect from an adult who has just discovered a new facial feature. I had given it to our daughter.

"Ok, but what's so special about it?"

"It's pretty," she told me. "And it makes it easier to put on eyeliner."

"Huh," I said.

I guess I was aware that the eyes of East Asians are different from those of Westerners, but I hadn't given much thought to how or why. In all humans, the eyelid is opened by a tiny muscle called the *levator palpebrae superioris*, which starts out as a cordlike structure on the front of the skull and becomes wider and flatter as it continues downward, looking a bit like a cat o' nine tails as it splits into numerous fibers; this is collectively called the *levator aponeurosis*. These fibers connect to the tarsal plate, a dense connective tissue structure that forms the rigid scaffold for the eyelid. In Westerners, some of the fibers also attach to the skin, resulting in a supratarsal crease when the eye is opened. In about fifty percent of East Asians, these connections to the skin are absent. This allows the normal fat behind the eyelid to slide a little further down, erasing the crease. *Sankapul*, then, comes down to the quirks of a tiny muscle and its attachments.

The surgery to correct the Asian eyelid was first described in 1896 by a Japanese surgeon named Mikamo. He discovered that he could create a convincing double eyelid by marking a line about six-to-eight millimeters above the margin of the eyelid and passing sutures along this line, through the eyelid conjunctiva and tarsal plate. He published his findings about forty-three years after American naval officer Commodore Matthew Perry arrived on Japanese shores—backed up by a fleet of gunboats—in order to force the historically cloistered country into foreign trade. As Japan opened to the West, it was flooded by new technology, habits, and ideas on the meaning of femininity and beauty. It was also introduced to more permissive attitudes towards cosmetic surgery.

It is telling to read different opinions about what, exactly, the purpose of this surgery was. The cynic in me sees a straight line between Perry's gunships and the concept of *sankapul*: both expressions of power. Mikamo, on the other hand, seemed to reject the notion that his invention was intended to emulate the appearance of Western women. In fact, he wrote that about eighty percent of the Japanese population had a double eyelid anyway, and that the single eyelid imparted a look that was "monotonous and impassive." Moreover, the single eyelid did not conform to "what writers and painters have regarded as an indicator of beauty."

There was very little written about Mikamo's surgery for a few decades after his original article. However, as East Asian countries became richer and more cosmopolitan, the volume of medical literature on the topic increased. Asian blepharoplasty, as Mikamo's surgery became known, has become one of the most popular cosmetic procedures in Taiwan and South Korea. It has also become widely available in the United States, as Asian immigration has increased, and is now one of the most common surgeries for Asians in the United States. Medical articles in the 1980s described the procedure in terms of the "Westernization" of the Asian eyelid. As this term fell out of favor, more recent articles emphasize the importance of maintaining an ethnically appropriate look.

It is now more common to see the surgery promoted as a procedure to decrease the appearance of tiredness, confer the appearance of alertness, and make it easier to apply eyeliner. Instead of assigning diminished value to a single eyelid, surgeons now medicalize it, cloaking the procedure in the value-free language of science. It allows the patient and surgeon to worry more about the technical aspects of the procedure without being caught up in what, if anything, is being created or erased.

I felt like all this history had landed rather unfairly on my daughter's face. But at the moment, I wasn't worried about this. At the moment, I was locked in an endless battle of attrition between me and my baby. It was my turn to put her to bed.

We had decided to paint our nursery a gender-neutral dark gray color. The large window in the east wall of the room was blacked out to facilitate, largely theoretical, afternoon naps. When the lights were turned out, the room was illuminated only by a set of icy white LED nightlights, and the whole room took on an ethereal bluish hue. It was around 3:45 am. As long as I held the baby and rocked her, she stayed quiet. But as soon as I attempted to lay her in her crib, the screaming started, and I was reduced to picking her back up and resuming my rocking.

The blue room was sealed off from the world outside. Light and noise were blocked out. The clock was invisible in the dark. I stood in the center bouncing, bouncing. Most new parents—myself included—have never faced this kind of prolonged sleep deprivation, and I was not handling it well. The blue room was a brutal crucible in which a lifetime of accomplishments evaporated in the nightly physical struggle, where you were only as valuable as your ability to put the baby down.

I tried not to think about the time. The prospect of going to work on two or three hours of sleep made a small bead of sweat emerge on my forehead. Exhausted, I decided that I wasn't standing anymore and sat down in our chair, trying to keep rocking. She raised her arms over her head, the tips of her tiny fingers only barely reaching the top. And that was the last thing I remembered because we both fell, blessedly, asleep.

In the first three months of parenthood, nights melt into days as everyone just tries to stay fed, clothed, and bathed. On one hazy morning during that time, I sat in our living room watching TV, having settled on a reality show on cross-cultural relationships. Coincidentally, the subjects were a white man who had married a Korean woman. The filmmakers followed them as they prepared for their son's *dol*, the traditional Korean one-year birthday celebration.

The *dol* is a big deal, a holdover from the times when a significant number of babies in Korea didn't see their first birthday. The climax of the celebration is the *doljabi*, a ritual in which several artifacts are placed around the infant, each one signifying a particular life path. Food may mean a life of plenty. A ball of string may signify a long life. A book may represent smarts. Then, surrounded by a throng of camera-wielding friends and family, each yelling words of encouragement or discouragement, the child is left to pick up the object that predicts her future.

In the show, the husband was being interviewed. He was happily discussing how plans were going for the upcoming *dol*. He touched on the venue, the decorations, the guest list, etc. Eventually, the subject of the *doljabi* came up. He talked about when they would do it and what items their son would be choosing from. When asked what he hoped his son would choose, he paused. He looked away, and his face fell. After a few seconds, he looked back at the camera, his eyes wet, and he resumed speaking, his voice now cracking.

"I just … I just … want him to be happy," he said, choking up.

A few moments later the scene switched to the mother's family. The father's tears were never explored further, and in later scenes, he seemed as good-natured as ever.

What was with the sudden emotion? Why was he crying? For me, the scene was like tasting a familiar spice that I couldn't name. I identified with his emotion, but I couldn't articulate an explanation.

I didn't discuss the show with my wife. In fact, when she found out what I was writing about, a look of sudden annoyance briefly crossed her face. Like when you realize the grape you are eating is not seedless.

"You can't fucking write about *sankapul*," she told me.

"Why not?"

"Because you are not Asian."

"But I am Asian," I argued.

There was that look again—followed by this:

"Well … no one ever called you 'chinky eyes' when you were growing up."

I had never heard her use that slur before, and it was shocking to hear it from her. I was powerless to argue, because she was right. I had no skin in the game. I would never feel the violence of those words, and could never rightfully criticize the longing of people who tried to escape from under them.

"People tell me that my eyes are beautiful like they are. They ask me why I would ever want to change them. Those people always have huge eyes and perfect *sankapul*. They don't know…"

But it wasn't true that I had no stake in this. Because even though I would never be called "chinky eyes," my daughter would always be noted for her *sankapul*. And *sankapul* was chinky eyes' counterpart. They drew their power from one another.

Back in the blue room, my own desperation gave rise to some fanciful thoughts. I thought about how I stood no chance in my struggle with this incomprehensibly complicated thing. This baby must be fitted with sophisticated instruments, ready to sound the alarm if she was lowered into her crib. A little too much roll, pitch, or yaw in my incompetent hands, and she would start screaming again.

So I kept rocking. Kept bouncing. Wanting to cry. Thinking about crying. Thinking about the crying father on the television show. Wanting his child to be happy. Contemplating what that meant. Our baby was two months old now. Sooner than we could imagine, it would be time for her one-year birthday. Time for her *doljabi*. And it would be up to us to pick out the artifacts which she would navigate to determine her future.

Would she be smart? Savvy enough to avoid the most obvious shiny thing? Did she have a chance? Would she pick the microphone of an entertainer? The pen of a writer? How about the fake money which signified a job in business or finance?

I wish I could help her navigate the sheet, scattered as it would be by all sorts of unforeseen objects. Perry's warships would be placed far out of the way. So would Mikamo's scalpel. There would be people gathered around, yelling impassive, monotonous, *sankapul*, or chinky eyes. I would place those people forever out of earshot.

I was beginning to understand the other father's reaction to his son's *doljabi*. The ritual was an act of unfettered agency: A child left alone to crawl around and pick up toys. Maybe the dad's tears were an acknowledgement of the naïveté, the heartbreaking innocence of that. And perhaps, also, the father's tears were tears of sadness. A recognition that the *doljabi* was a one-off. No matter who we were, our babies would grow up and find out that pure self-determination would always be attenuated by the inescapable past.

I accidentally bobbled the baby and she stirred. In spite of my efforts to soothe her, an invariable sequence had begun, and she started to whimper, bear down, turn bright red, and scream. Anna knocked on the door and asked if I needed any help. I sleepily nodded "yes" and she got ready to feed the baby. In the meantime, I bounced the baby over my left shoulder—the position that seemed to work best to calm her down.

But she continued to scream, and was even able to lift her head a little so that she could turn and shriek directly into my ear. Despite the malevolent intent of this maneuver, it forced her to brush the five-day stubble of my cheek with the incredible softness of her own. This was when I loved her most. When she was at her loudest, making her demands known, finding her voice already.

PLAYS

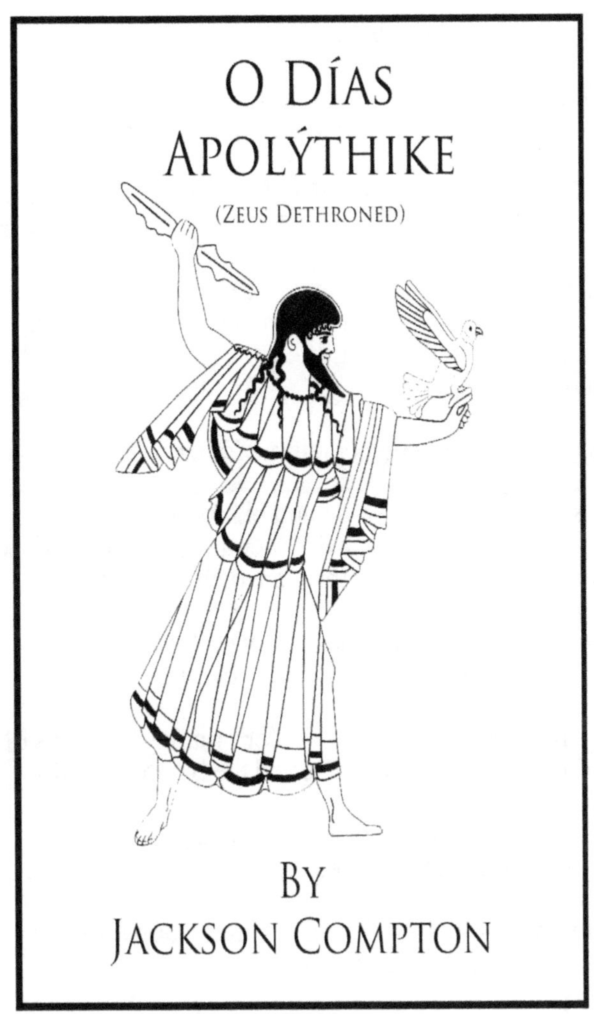

ARTWORK BY PLAYWRIGHT, JACKSON COMPTON

Cast of Characters

Zeus: Ruler of the Greek Gods on Mount Olympus.
Husband to Hera. Known for his unfaithful trysts with
goddesses and humans alike.

Hera: Jealous wife of Zeus. Goddess of sacred marriage.
Known for tormenting Zeus's lovers and progeny.

Hades: God of the Underworld and keeper of dead souls.
Husband to Persephone.

Persephone: Goddess of spring. Wife to Hades, daughter of
Zeus and Demeter. Spends nine months of the year in the
realm of Hades and the other three months with her mother
on Mount Olympus.

Demeter: Goddess of cereal grains. Mother of Persephone.

Hephaestus: God of craftsmen and blacksmiths. Husband to
Aphrodite, son of Hera. Known for crafting weapons of the
gods and goddesses and the throne which snared Hera.

Aphrodite:Goddess of passion and love. Wife to Hephaestus.
Known for enraging the lusts of god and man alike.

Hermes: Messenger God. Known for bringing the souls of
the dead to the Underworld. Created the lyre for Apollo.

Athena: Goddess of wisdom and war. Daughter of Zeus.
Known for having sprung from Zeus's head fully grown.

Ares: God of war. Son of Zeus and Hera. Known for the
violent and physical parts of war.

Artemis: Goddess of the hunt. Twin sister to Apollo,
daughter of Zeus and the Titaness Leto. Known as the
Eternal Virgin.

Apollo: God of the sun, music and poetry. Twin brother
to Artemis, son of Zeus and the Titaness Leto. Known for
leading the Muses.

<u>Poseidon</u>: God of the sea. Brother to Zeus. Known for his terrible temper.

<u>Dionysus</u>: God of grape-harvest, wine, fertility, ritual madness, and Greek theater.

<u>Charon</u>: Ferryman of the dead over the River Styx into the realm of Hades.

<u>Souls of the Dead</u>: Those waiting to cross the River Styx into the realm of Hades.

<u>Chorus</u>: The nine Muses of Apollo.

<u>Brief Summary</u>

The Greek Gods and Goddesses find themselves changed into mortals. As they gather together at the base of Mount Olympus, accusations fly as to who is responsible for causing such degrading blasphemy.

<u>Setting</u>

In the realm of Hades, along the River Styx, and at the base of Mount Olympus.

<u>Time</u>

Some time after the Heroic Age.

ACT I
Scene 1

SETTING: Throne room of Hades and Persephone in the Underworld.

AT RISE: HADES and PERSEPHONE sit on their respective thrones on a dais. PERSEPHONE, regal as always. HADES, looking dire, almost bored. The entry door swings open. CHARON briskly ENTERS, marching to the dais and kneels before the King and Queen.

CHORUS

We the Muses give voice to the story set before you, beginning in the realm of Hades where the King and his Queen, Persephone, rule the Underworld.

PERSEPHONE

This is a first. To what do we owe the honor of your presence, Charon?

HADES

Why have you abandoned your post, Ferryman? Who ushers in the dead in your absence?

CHARON

No one, my lord. The Styx has shallowed and the boat is grounded on this side of the river. It's as if the waters are draining away.

PERSEPHONE

Is that even possible, Husband?

(HADES rises from the throne and takes PERSEPHONE'S hand.)

HADES

Show us.

(CHARON turns, followed by HADES and PERSEPHONE. They EXIT the hall.)

(BLACKOUT)
(END OF SCENE)

<u>ACT I</u>
<u>Scene 2</u>

SETTING: Bank of what is left of the River Styx. The Ferryman's boat is beached and listing on its side on the bank

AT RISE: HADES, PERSEPHONE, and CHARON ENTER.

CHARON

The river is vanishing. It's practically gone now.

PERSEPHONE

Why, it's so shallow anyone could walk across it.

HADES

And so we shall. Ferryman, your place is with your boat.

CHARON

As you wish, my King.

(A fog rises, obscuring CHARON on the far bank.HADES and PERSEPHONE proceed to cross, where the river had once been, to the opposite bank where the DEAD SOULS wait.The DEAD SOULS crowd around HADES and PERSEPHONE.)

DEAD SOUL

(holding out his hand offering two obols)
Here are my coins for passage.

(HADES ignores the offering. He surveys the surroundings.)

DEAD SOUL

Please! My coins for passage, as is my right!
(The crowd presses in, all offering their coins. PERSEPHONE is jostled by the onslaught and somewhat startled.)

PERSEPHONE

Husband! Let us away to our chambers! We must cross back over the river.

HADES

The Styx is gone. There's no river to cross. We are blocked from our
realm

PERSEPHONE

Impossible!

HADES

Wife, do you not feel its absence? Our lack of power? Gods we are no
longer.

PERSEPHONE

What then? Are we mortals? Or something else entirely? What are we
to do?

HADES

Seek our answers elsewhere. Stand aside, shades, and let your king and
queen pass. Your coins buy no passage, so long as the Styx remains dry.

(The crowd parts, leaving a path. PERSEPHONE takes HADES' arm,
and the pair sets off for the entrance into the Underworld.)

(BLACKOUT)
(END OF SCENE)

<u>ACT I</u>
<u>Scene 3</u>

SETTING: At the base of Mount Olympus.

AT RISE: ZEUS ENTERS, tumbling down the mountainside, end over end, coming to a bumpy stop at the base of Mount Olympus. His once-powerful lightning bolt has changed into a jagged representation of itself, looking more like a zigzag walking stick. He is nicked with cuts and bruises.

CHORUS
And so it came to pass that the Gods on High fell to the earth as mortals. Even Zeus, Father of the Olympian Gods, was not exempted from the heinous act.

ZEUS
(holding his head and staggering to his feet)
By my own oath! What has come to pass? What enemy is upon us? Have the Titans once again been loosed to wreak havoc? I've no memory of such a happening.
(Zeus shades his eyes and looks up at the summit of Mount Olympus.)
Cast down from my perch on Mount Olympus where only eagles dare fly with the Gods?
(Looking at the scrapes and blood on his arms.)
Where is the ichor so soon replaced by this ruby nectar, flowing so freely from these wounds? Only men are doomed to bleed so.

(ATHENA ENTERS wearing her splendid armor.)

ATHENA
Fare thee well, Father? You are wounded!

ZEUS
Nay, dear Daughter Athena. Merely scratches. My pride took the brunt of the fall and therein lies the real hurt. Truthfully, I ached more so when you sprang forth from my own head—fully grown!

ATHENA
(staring into the distance, shielding her eyes from the sun)
Father, someone or something approaches from the distant sky.

ZEUS

If it be foe, this thunderbolt forged by the Cyclopes has lost all its spark.

ATHENA

No Father, not an enemy, but a friend. The Messenger, Hermes!

(HERMES ENTERS, flying, landing heavily on the ground.)

HERMES

My wings, though adequate enough to reach the base of Mount Olympus, go no higher. Luckily, here wait Athena and father Zeus.

ZEUS

Whence have you come, Hermes, son of mine?

HERMES

One instant guiding souls to Hades' realm, when next I fell from the heavens near the altar of my own shrine in sweet Arcadia. The strength of my wings much lessened from head and toe, yet still I flew, though ever fearful of Icarus's precipice.

ATHENA

Wise decision, Hermes, for with these forms so lately entered, one misstep could be an undoing. Fly no higher than you must.

HERMES

Know you anything of this happening?

ATHENA

Not the cause, only the symptom.

ZEUS

To which the answers are withheld. Rest only a moment, Hermes, then take flight! Search the land and skies for our kin!

HERMES

My wings being not as they once were, I'm to question such a task, Father.

ATHENA

Agreed. Ill-advised for such perilous travels. Father?

ZEUS

It is as commanded, Daughter. Seek the others, Hermes.

HERMES

As you command, my lord.
(HERMES gives a stiff bow.)

ATHENA

May the Fates keep your thread safe! Fare thee well, Hermes!

HERMES

Thank you, wise and noble one.
(HERMES nods to Athena and takes to the sky, EXITING.)

ZEUS

Don't look at me in such a way, Daughter. Soften your gaze, for we
know not what we're up against. Necessary risks must be taken. Rulers
are destined for such dire decision making.

ATHENA

As you say, Father. Hark! Another approaches!

(DIONYSUS ENTERS, appearing on the hillside, wreath of grapevine
at an odd tilt on his head. His clothes are disheveled and torn. Claw
marks cover his body. He carries a dented gold wine cup in one hand.)

DIONYSUS

Surely voices were heard? Ah! Here are Father Zeus and my fellow
parthenogenous offspring, Athena!

CHORUS

Metis might argue that point, just as Semele should on your behalf,
Dionysus.

ZEUS

Why are you beaten so, God of the Vine? Tell me such.

DIONYSUS

Damnedest thing, Father! My constant companions, both leopard and
panther, forgot themselves! With a rush of raked claws, together they
disappeared quickly into the forest! If only these wounds leaked with
the juice of the sweet grapes it resembles!

ZEUS

Where do you come you from, Dionysus?

DIONYSUS

From wherever I last went, though only the gods know for sure.

ZEUS

Know you what's happened?

DIONYSUS

Only travesty, Father! No longer does my cup runneth over. Poor me!
(DIONYSUS turns the empty wine cup over and drops it to the
ground.)
Alas—I'm in need of drink! How must anyone function so without it?

ATHENA

Better luck you'd have conversing with his cup, Father, for no answers
will you find here. Though all is not lost, for others come up the hill.

(APHRODITE, barely clothed, and ARES, fully armored, ENTER.
Both clamber up the hill, arguing with one another.)

APHRODITE

Easier said of you, Ares! For covered you are in protection. Never was
a goddess meant for such traveling. Whosoever cursed Man with the
penance of walking, tell me true, God of War?

ARES

Protection it may be, Aphrodite, but it is heavy as the World resting on
Atlas's own shoulders! Never has my armor felt so until this very day, for
labored and short are my steps, so easily should the Goddess of Love
keep up with them.

APHRODITE

Behold, 'tis Zeus! Deservéd this punishment is not! I demand you
release me from these earthly chains! Immediately!

ARES

Lost you your sight, leaving only complaints in its place? Look again,
Aphrodite, for your chains are his own.

ZEUS

'Tis true, Son. A mortal's fate we all shall face, unless the nature of this scheme reveals itself.

APHRODITE

Has it not? This scheme is in accordance with your own actions, Zeus the Almighty, whether your hand was directly in it or not!

ZEUS

What say you in justification for such accusation?

APHRODITE

If only there were another eternity to air all such grievances against you.

CHORUS

One eternity most certainly be not enough!

ZEUS

How dare you speak to me so, Aphrodite? I'm ruler of the gods!

APHRODITE

Because I'm not your sibling nor progeny, though created am I from your own treachery! Born from the froth of blood spilled into the sea from the very genitals of your father, Cronus, cut from him by your own hand! Deny it so?

ZEUS

I deny it not! That tale has not been forgotten, nor have the wars against the Titans, for they are known by all! I ask again—what say you, that I be the cause indirectly or not, of this happening?

APHRODITE

Many enemies have you made over the years, Lord Zeus. Many wait in remembrance.

(HERA ENTERS.)

HERA

Do tell, Goddess of Love and Desire. Who has my husband wronged, more so than his own wife?

ZEUS

Hera! Queen of the gods! Glad are mine own eyes seeing you again!

CHORUS

Rarely, though that be the case!

HERA

That sounded almost sincere, Husband. Why? Are you lacking in young maidens to indulge your lustful fancies?

ZEUS

As I've said before, and to my bitter shame...responsible is Aphrodite for the all-consuming madness inflicted upon me which caused such utter degradation, for no god willingly consorts with humans in such a manner!

CHORUS

Then who were Ganymede, Lysithea, Pandora, Protogenia, Thyia, Antiope, Callisto, Libya, Nioba, Cassiopeia, Danae, Elara, Dia, Eurymedousa, Lalyke, Olympias, Lamia, Pyrrha, and Phthia?

ZEUS

My will was not my own!

APHRODITE

(laughing)
Use me as an excuse all you want, Zeus. Truth is, my guiles were used on you once, twice at most. Your own lustfulness did your bidding without me!

ZEUS

Completely untrue!

HERA

I'm inclined to believe her, oh husband of mine. How many forms have you taken on to sow your oats with human kind? At least a dozen to my knowledge, though I'm sure there's been dozens more.

CHORUS

Fifty-seven, by our reckoning, but who's counting?

HERA

An army of sons and daughters you've fathered. Though in this new form, your disguises may not be so convincing as they once were.

ZEUS

Wife, your words wound me so.

HERA

And every offspring you've created without me is an even deeper
wound for me to bear! Complain not of your offense, husband, for it is
nothing compared to the hurt of mine own!

ZEUS

Your anger is evident. I've no words for a defense.

APHRODITE

Hera, your spite of Zeus spills over on the rest of us! Why are we all
made to suffer so?

HERA

Surely I'm not to be blamed for what has happened? Where's my
knowledge of such arts? For my skills lie elsewhere.

APHRODITE

Perhaps not, but still convinced am I that Zeus lies at the heart of the
problem. That is, unless you still harbor ill will for Eris' Golden Apple
awarded to me by the young Trojan prince, Paris?
Aphrodite holds up the Golden Apple inscribed, "For the Fairest."

HERA

Athena is just as inclined, because she too was a contestant.

ATHENA

True. Though bribery alone won that contest. To Paris, Aphrodite
offered the most beautiful human woman, the fair Helen of Sparta.

APHRODITE

Indeed. But as I remember it, we all bribed him. And no man is
unsusceptible to his heart's desire.

HERA

As evident by my husband's infidelity.

ATHENA

My head rules over such matters, for wisdom dwells not in the heart.
Grudges are for lesser beings.

CHORUS

Tell that to Medusa and Arachne.

(ARTEMIS and APOLLO, both carrying bows with knocked arrows, and HERACLES, carrying his club, ENTER.)

HERACLES

I never needed a bow for my Twelve Labors, Artemis. A club worked fine.

CHORUS

Ask Achilles which of the two slayed him.

ARTEMIS

Look there, Brother Apollo. Our kin stand on the edge of Mount Olympus. Their troubles appear to be our own.

APOLLO

Hark, fellow Olympians! Knowest thou what ails the lot? Tell me, Father Zeus, what has become of us?

ZEUS

I know not, Son. No answers have I for you or anyone else.

(DEMETER ENTERS.)

DEMETER

Tell me, have we all truly succumbed to human mortality? Know you of the whereabouts of my daughter, Persephone?

ATHENA

As can only be guessed. Persephone has yet to make an appearance, Demeter, Mother of the Grains. Though the realm of Hades is far off and not without its dangers.

ARES

Ho! Hermes comes, carrying the Lame God!

(HERMES ENTERS flying low to the ground carrying, Hephaestus)

HERMES

Never have my winged helmet and sandals worked so hard, Hephaestus!

HEPHAESTUS

Praise to you, Hermes! Without your means of flight, I'd still be stuck
on the mountainside of Lemnos. My leg is more useless now than ever
before!

HERA

If it isn't my son, the blacksmith. If ever someone was capable of such a
happening, it would be you, Hephaestus!

HEPHAESTUS

Mother, so little do you think of me? I'm the architect of all the heavenly
palaces in which each of us resides. I've created wonders of every
conceivable desire. Every piece of functioning perfection coveted by
all. What good am I, being mortal? Where's the beauty in the finite? For
what purpose would that serve?

HERA

Your moments of pettiness are well known. I've experienced it firsthand.

CHORUS

Hera is an expert on such matters!

HEPHAESTUS

Still, are you angry about the throne constructed to immobilize you in
its chains?

HERA

Such an act was disrespectful to the Queen of Heaven! Leaving me to
be laughed at and ridiculed by all the others!

HEPHAESTUS

No more than you deserved, false Mother! You hurled me from the peak
of Mount Olympus at Aphrodite's urging, I was only a baby—crashing
down onto the rocky shore! Yet Thetis raised me as her own, showing
love where none had been given from you! More a mother is she than
you could ever be to anyone!

ARES

Hold thy tongue, twisted little man! That's also my mother you speak so
harshly against!

HEPHAESTUS
Ares, you truly are Hera's successor, and rightfully so.

ARES
My arms would make you speak a different story!

HEPHAESTUS
The very arms and armor which I made for you? Wearing them as you
wear my own wife, War God? Known to me are all of Aphrodite's
indiscretions. If ever revenge were a motive, it would be deservedly
mine. However, of this particular account, I am wholly innocent of such
responsibility.

APHRODITE
I was gifted as your wife by Zeus's will alone! That agreement was
never my own, yet bear it, I must! If ever there was an excuse to hate
Zeus, it is only one of many!

ZEUS
My right as a Father determines who my daughters marry!
(ZEUS angrily hurls his zig-zag thunder bolt away, stabbing it in the
ground near Athena. ATHENA removes the bolt from the ground,
studying it.)

APHRODITE
Only your might as a god curved my will, for I am no daughter of
yours! And in this current state, I will speak my mind and do as I please,
loving whom I will love!

ZEUS
I alone rule this realm! All will do as commanded!

HERA
Has all wisdom leaped from your head, husband? The world is not as
we left it! Different rules must be applied.

(POSEIDON ENTERS, climbing up the hillside.)

ZEUS
Tell me Poseidon, were the three realms not divided equally among
us by lots? You ruled over the seas, while Hades ruled over the
Underworld, leaving me the heavens in the sky above?

POSEIDON

As you say, Brother. The heavens are not your only domain, for you
rule over all the gods as well, though none ever gave you leave to do so.
Your might set our own boundaries, and none had will or power enough
to question the authority of Zeus almighty without opposition.

ZEUS

Though now seems the opportune time for just such a moment?

POSEIDON

We are all equals in mortality, Brother. You deserve the wrath.

ZEUS

So, this is how everyone perceives their lord? Only as a tyrant and a
lecherous beast?

CHORUS

Mostly a lecherous beast.

HERA

Your actions speak louder than words, Husband.

(HADES and PERSEPHONE enter together, arm in arm, gliding up
the hillside).

ZEUS

This scheme has reached as far as your own realm, Brother, Lord of
Hades?

HADES

The River Styx is no more, brothers. The power of oath and immortality
were tied to the river.

HEPHAESTUS

I shall prove my innocence of so much wrong doing, Mother, and
search out the cause for this dilemma. Maybe then you'll think better of
me! Hermes, if your wings can still fly for the both of us, aid me in the
journey to Hades realm to solve this riddle!

HERMES

My wings will try for such a journey. I shall lead you into the Realm of
the Dead.

(HERMES carries Hephaestus away and EXITS.)

DEMETER
Persephone! My lovely daughter!

PERSEPHONE
Mother. I am relieved that you are well.

(DEMETER Runs to Persephone and embraces her.)

DEMETER
Joyful am I, seeing you again! No longer bound are you by the
pomegranate seeds eaten in the Underworld! You can stay the rest of
your mortal life with me!

PERSEPHONE
No, Mother. I will not. Here, I'm just a minor goddess, though in the
Underworld, I'm Queen of the Dead. I rule along with my husband who
I've learned to love. This is no longer my place.

(DEMETER grabs Persephone's hand with both of hers.)

DEMETER
Please, Daughter. All of this has been for you! Stay and live under my
wing so that we may take flight together. Please, stay alongside me.

PERSEPHONE
No, Mother!
(PERSEPHONE tries pulling away. DEMETER holds her fast.)
No! I will not stay with you!

DEMETER
Please, Daughter! I'm begging!

(PERSEPHONE yanks her hand free, stumbles backward, and falls,
striking her head hard against a stone on the ground.)

DEMETER
No! Persephone! Persephone! My sweet girl! What have I done?!
(DEMETER cradles the lifeless body of Persephone.)
Hera! It was not supposed to be this way! It's not as you promised me!

(HADES stares hard at his dead wife. He slowly turns and EXITS without a word.)

ZEUS

Are you behind this foiled plot, Wife? Who are your conspirators and to what end?

HERA

Yes! I admit it! Poseidon dammed the River Styx, though not knowing mortality awaited us all. Perhaps that was best for us all, for the only power available now is reason. Each god and goddess has some form of ill-will toward you for one thing or another. Even Aphrodite exemplifies the animosity for your actions, though she be not a conspirator in this scheme.

ZEUS

What would you have me do?

HERA

You are unworthy to rule the Gods! Apollo and Poseidon knew this years ago, and when they intervened, you forced them into human labors building the city walls of Troy. You did not listen to them. Without your might to force your will upon us all, you are now powerless. Yield, Husband! Yield, so that someone of worth may take your place ruling with a fair and just hand!

ZEUS

And who would that be, wife? Where's the wisdom and justice you seek? Who would be chosen in my absence? Who is more worthy to lead the gods?

(A surge of energy and a flash of light. ATHENA holds the thunderbolt of Zeus in both hands as the power rushes through her.)

HERA

My powers are restored! I'm a goddess once more!

ATHENA

Hephaestus must have dislodged the dam.
(ATHENA holds the thunderbolt high. Electrical discharges crackle from it.)
I've inherited your spark, Father, holding the power you once held.

HERA

Athena, you are the Goddess of Wisdom and Temperament. Perhaps you should take the mantel from mighty Zeus! 'Tis better this way. No one could ever accuse you of ulterior motives.

HERACLES

Agreed. Your wisdom and fairness abounds. Your reputation speaks with highest regards. I'll not go against, it if the others choose you.

(Most of the gods and goddesses nod in silent agreement.)

ZEUS

Perhaps this is for the best, Daughter. No other is such a worthy successor as you. If all agree, then so shall I.

ATHENA

We shall then travel to Mount Olympus shall we and discuss this further.

CHORUS

And so the gods and goddesses returned to Mount Olympus proper, and all were in rare agreement that Athena should rule with wisdom and just cause.

(BLACKOUT)
(END OF SCENE)

<u>ACT I</u>
<u>Scene 4</u>

SETTING: Bank of the River Styx.

AT RISE: CHARON ferries the dead across the river.
HADES ENTERS, surveying the order of the Underworld.

CHORUS

And so the Lord of the Dead returned to his realm.

(BLACKOUT)
(END OF SCENE)

<u>ACT I</u>
<u>Scene 5</u>

SETTING: Throne room of Hades and Persephone in the Underworld.

AT RISE: HADES ENTERS. PERSEPHONE is sitting on her throne.

PERSEPHONE

Welcome, Husband!

(HADES glides regally up the steps and sits next to Persephone, placing his hand on hers.)

PERSEPHONE

Husband, in death my entirety is now one with this realm. No longer will I leave you for months at a time. My mother's unknowing gift unites us forever.

HADES

What transpired above only serves us down below. All is as it should be, wife. Our love, eternal.

CHORUS

And so a New Age comes to pass over the world, and the voices of the Muses herald its arrival.

(BLACKOUT)
<u>THE END</u>

VISUAL ART

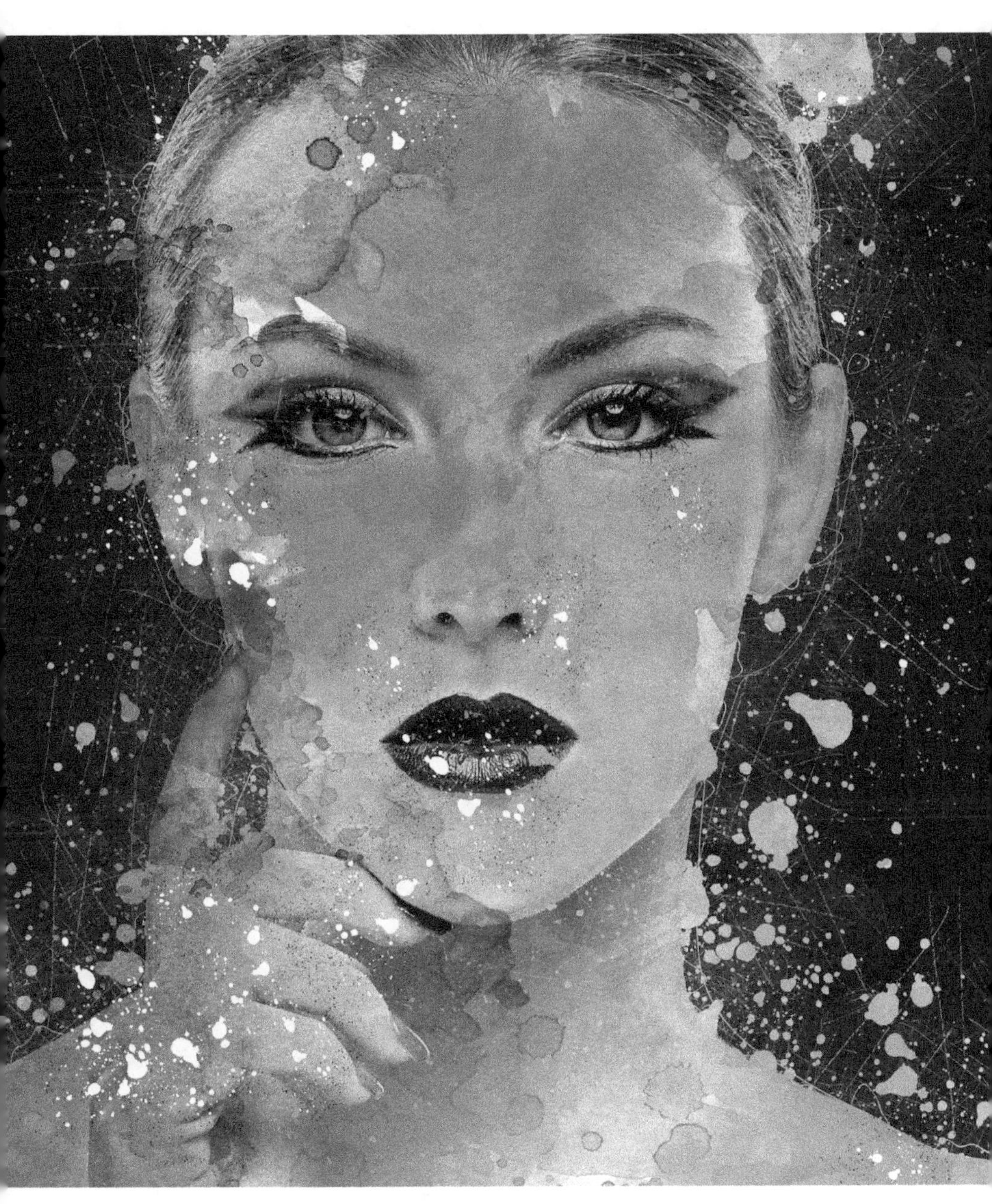

IMAGE BY BRIGITTE WERNER (CREATIVECOMMONS.ORG)

Untitled opus 2 no. 1

BY LIAO DEAN

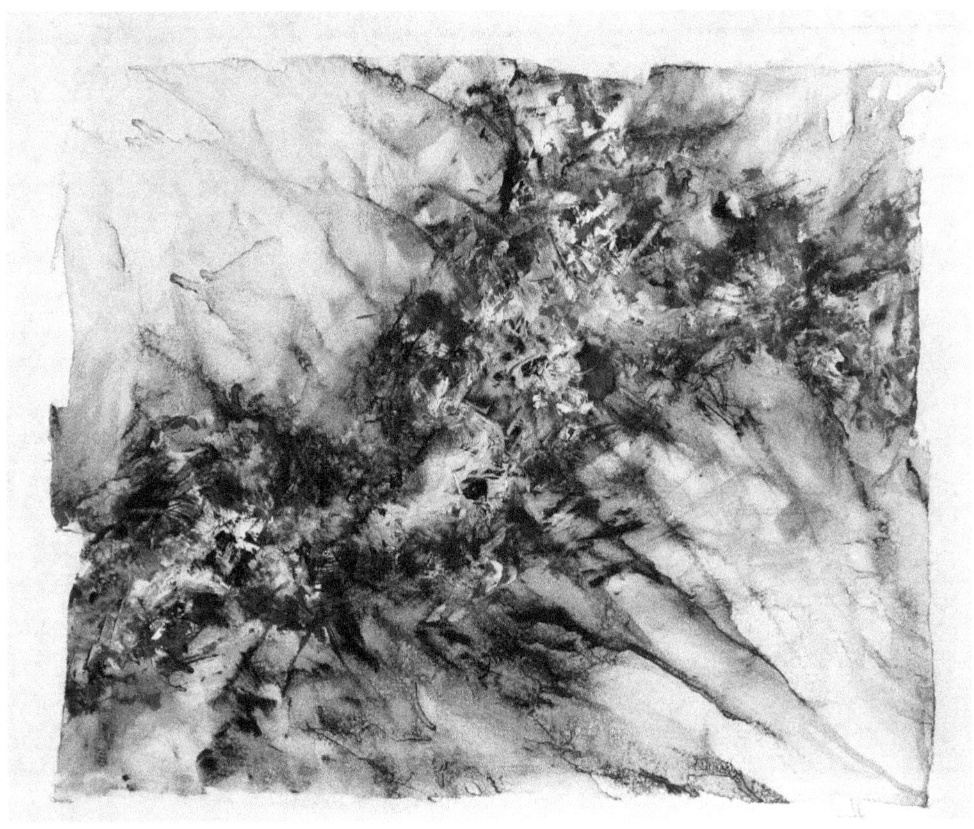

OIL AND CHARCOAL ON PAPER, 12 x 17in, 2018
Collection: Sanshui after Richter

5

BY JACOB NEWTON

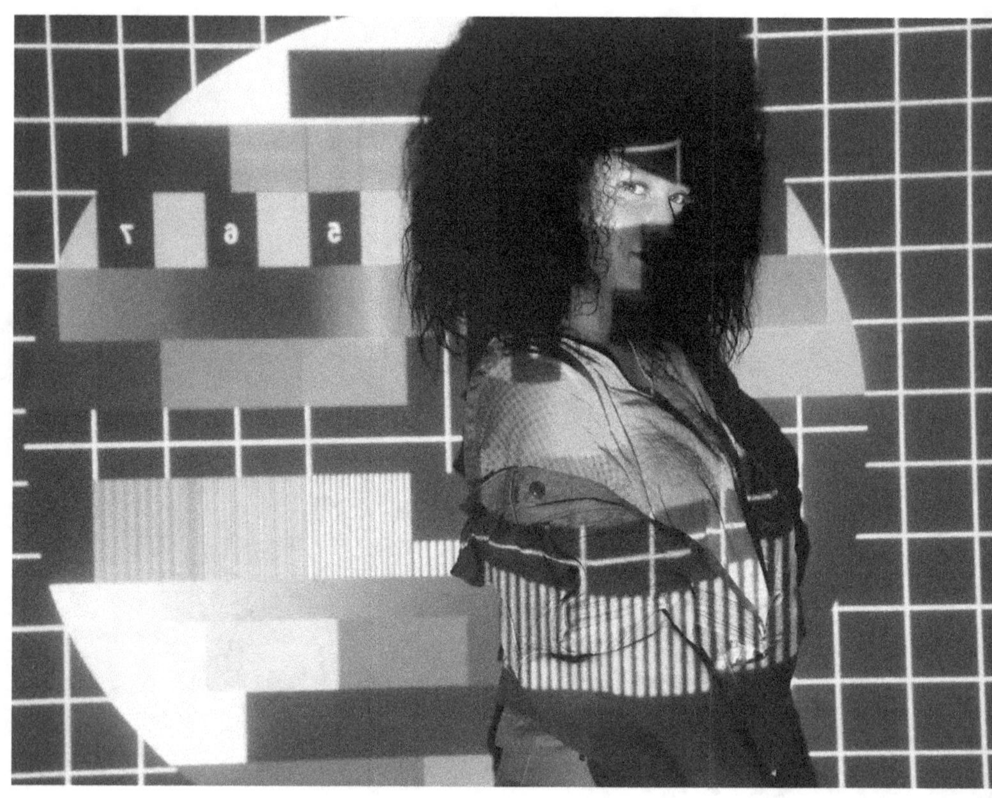

DIGITAL PHOTOGRAPH, 2018
Collection: Pigmented

Del Mar y sus Testigos

BY ESTEBAN JIMENEZ GUERRA

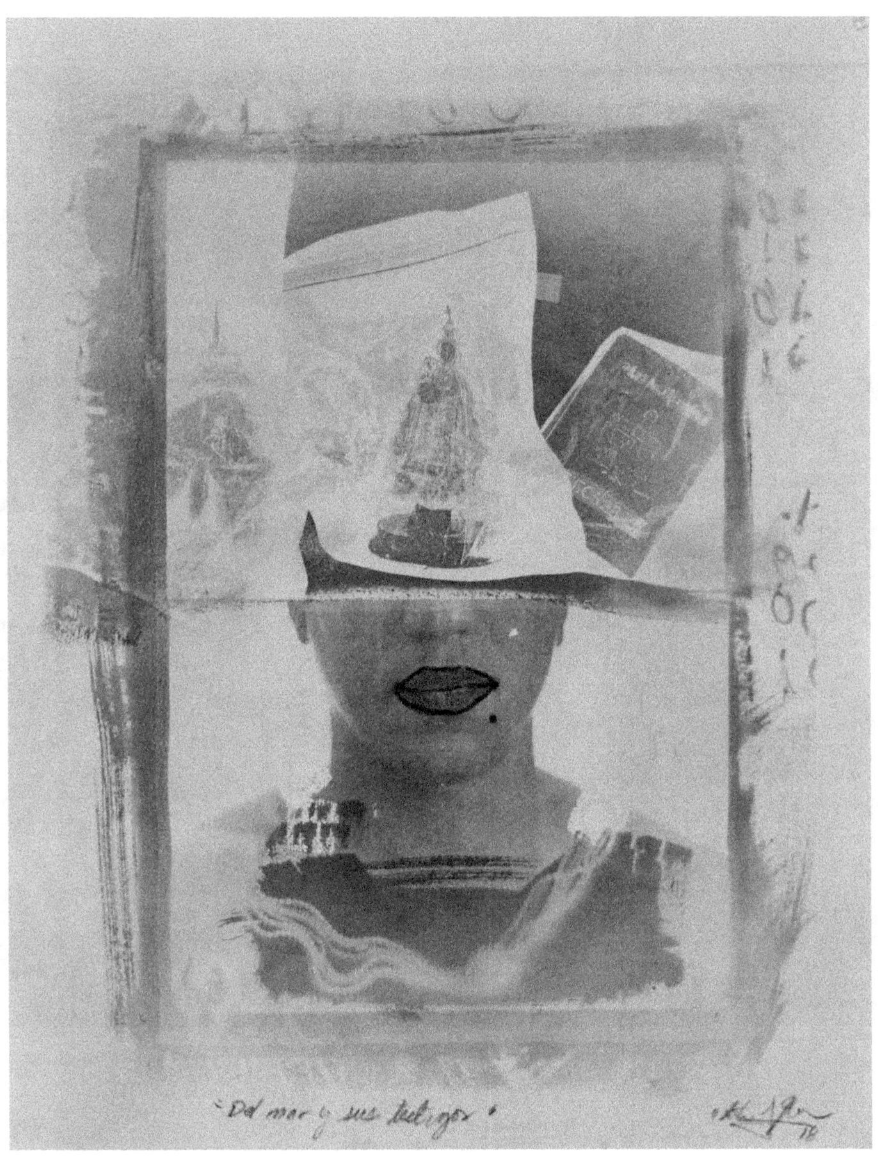

MIXED MEDIA ON CANVAS, 48 x48 in, 2018

Birds of boredom 2

BY RAMONA DARABANT

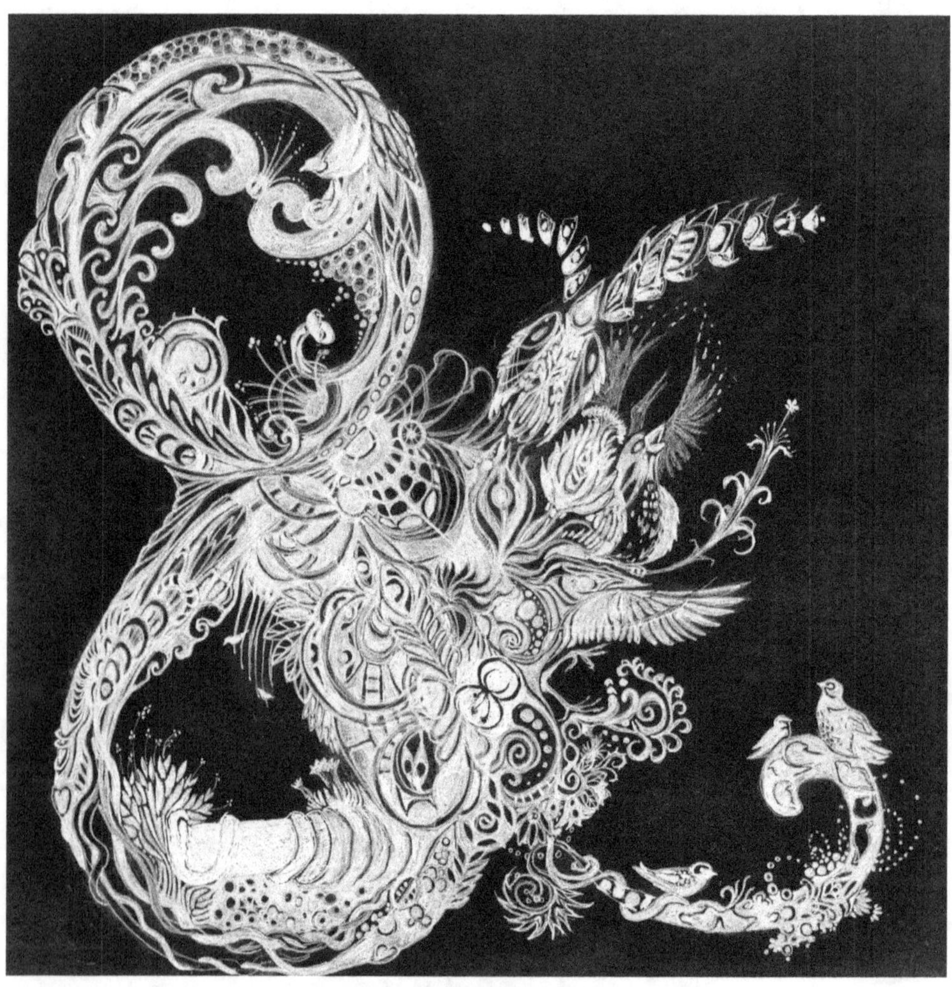

INK ON PAPER, 15 x 15 cm, 2014
Collection: Tales to Tell Myself

Diorama

BY JOSHUA ATLAS

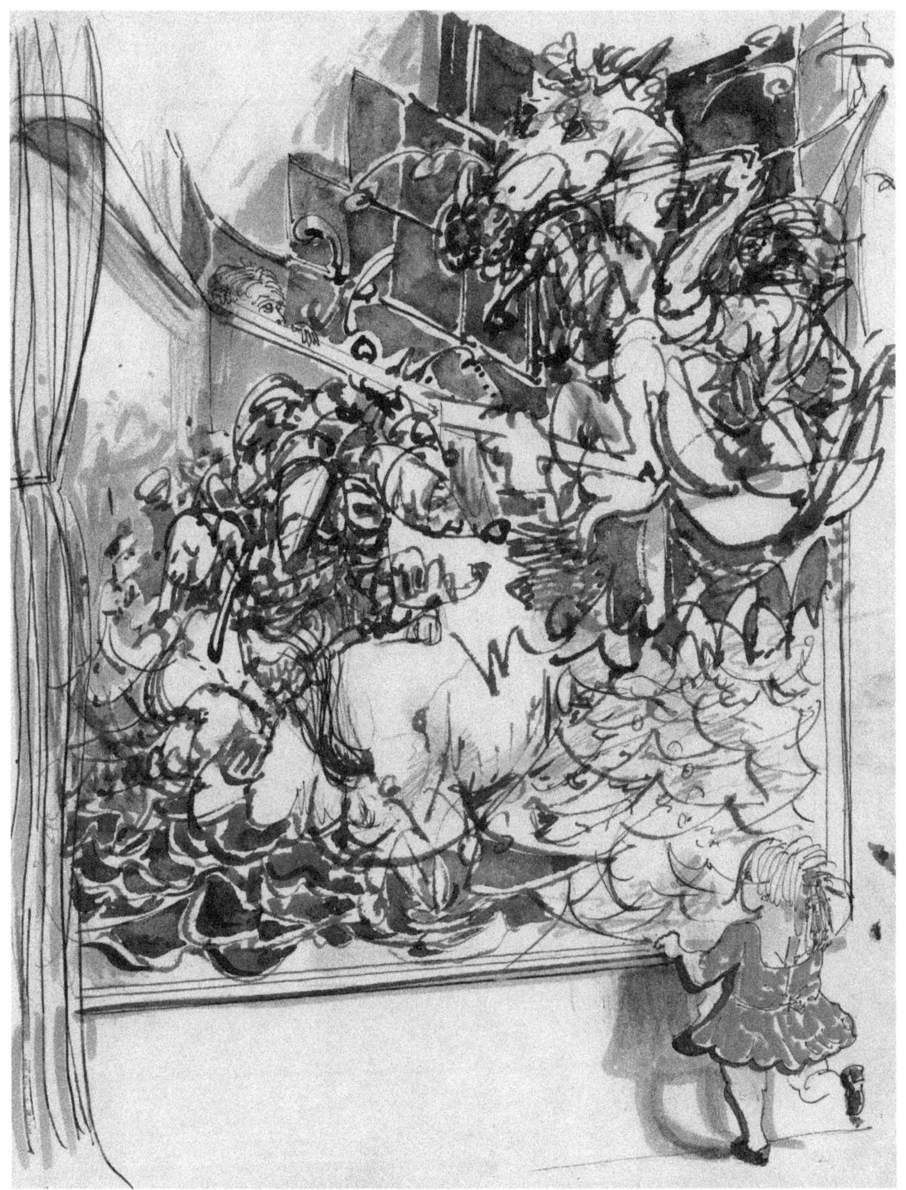

INK ON PAPER, 12 x 9 in, 2016

Realization

BY ESTEBAN JIMENEZ GUERRA

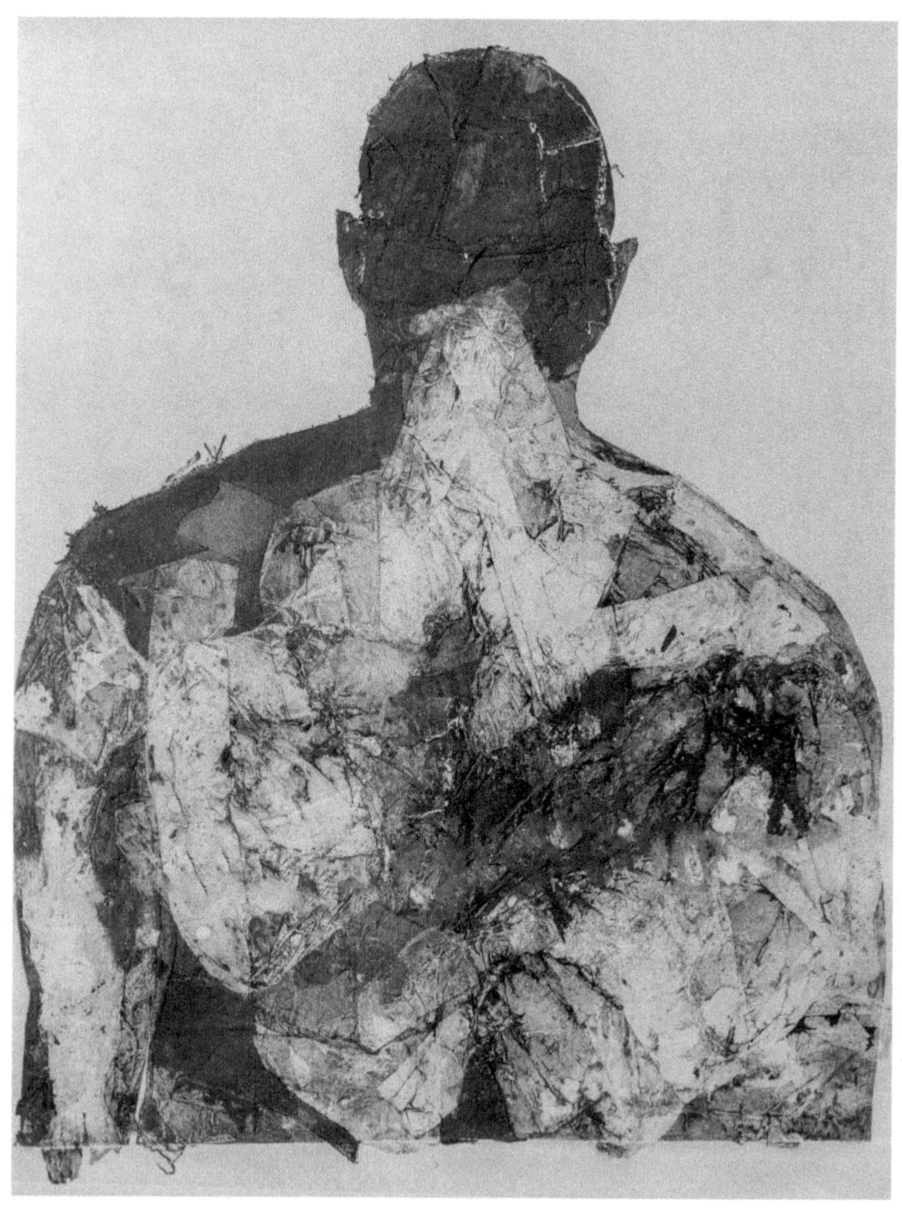

COLLAGRAPH ON BFK PAPER, 28 x 24 in, 2018

POETRY

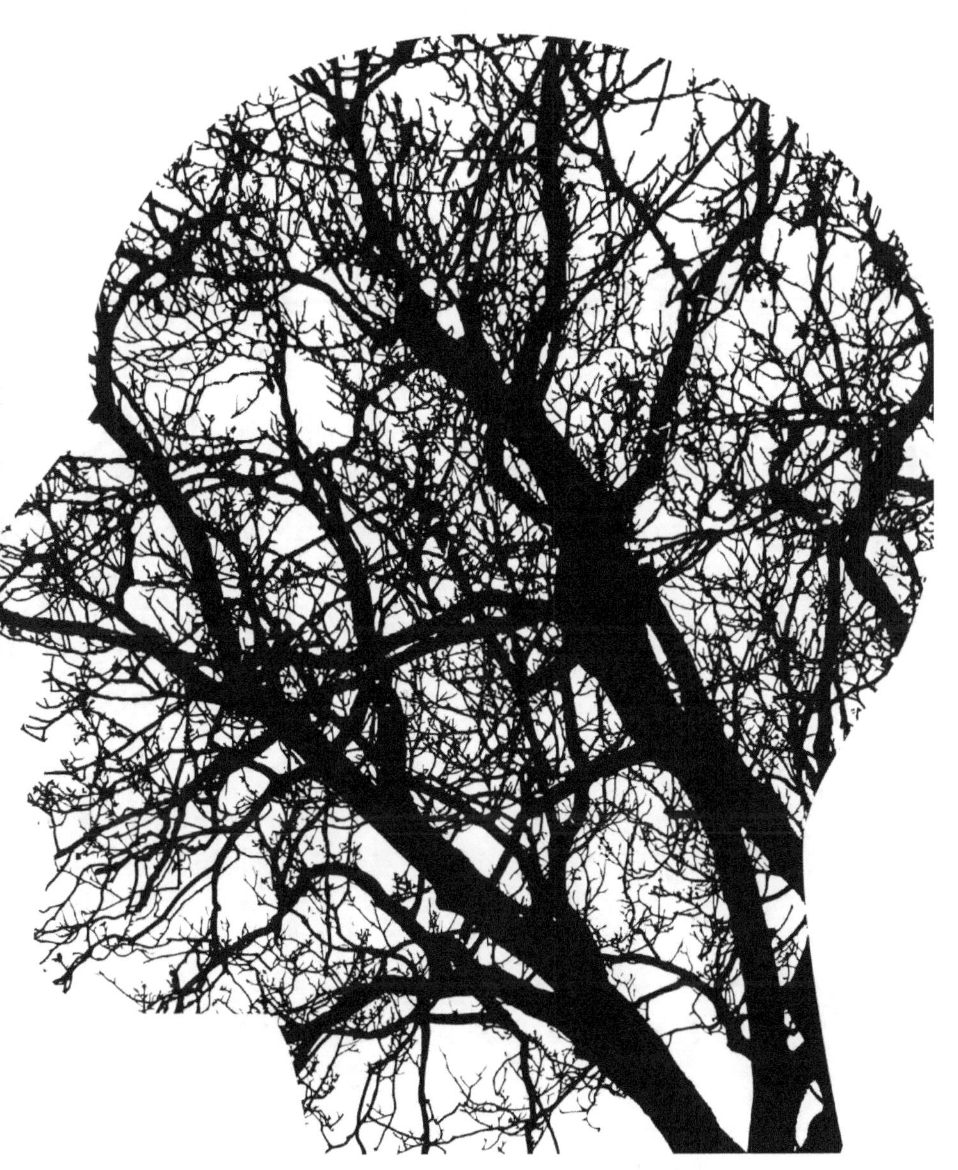

IMAGE BY GORDON JOHNSON (CREATIVECOMMONS.ORG)

Rosalba

BY ZOË BLAYLOCK

She began by walking toward each rising
sun with a basket filled with memories
wrapped in regrets, and a prayer worn
thin enough to tear.

Yearning to prevail, she sought peace
in living before finding it in dying.

For want of tranquil mind
she could have survived
muddled, or she could
have shrugged
and sighed.

But she wanted more.
She wanted more.

So, each morning, no matter how
tired or forlorn, she inched
toward the watery rising
-- thinking, reflecting,
hoping-- until
the knowing
came.

At first, she took it greedily, with
a clenched fist. Then with an
upward gaze and arms
spread wide.

And finally, fortunately, with her
head bowed, and an open palm.

Darkness of Crows

BY ANN HOWELLS

One for sorrow, two for mirth
three for a funeral, four for a birth
six for heaven, seven for hell,
eight for the Devil his own self.
       -Old English rhyme

Colored like rain-slick highways,
they must be hiding something. Nothing
so dark and sleek

can be innocent, and I suspect they sport
tattoos beneath those oiled feathers:
swastika, pentagram,

upside down cross. Unlovely
and unloved, they covet and thieve.
I watch them gather

like priests at the edge of the trees,
caw, caw, caw their rusty shrieks,
settle like sin

upon my shoulders. I kneel for absolution,
but there are not enough Hail Mary's
to save me.

Three Sisters

BY ANN HOWELLS

One flashes diamonds from every finger.
One thinks no one knows she drinks.
One forgets she has sisters.

One fears flying, snakes, and lightning.
One rubs tombstones in neglected graveyards.
One writes postcards to Mick Jagger.

One lives inside the novels of Jane Austen.
One recently took a lover.
One, perhaps more, is a congenital liar.

Uncle Charlie

BY RAYMOND P. HAMMOND

My great-uncle Charlie

Had no education

a bible inscribed by

      General Pershing

bad teeth which could

      be taken out (but sometimes

      he would forget to put back in)

a coal chute

a breakfast nook

a photo of a man in a coffin

      which he kept on top of the TV

a big wooden dresser which always had

      a carton of Doublemint chewing gum packs

      of which I would always get one

      because they were the next best thing

      to the block of chewing tobacco that he

      would cut chunks off with his pocket

knife, always holding the block in his

left hand while cupping it with his right

to draw the blade toward his

extended bent thumb

a photo of his two prized possessions,

a dog and a horse

He also became a ward of the state

after being diagnosed with "Hardening

of the arteries" taken from beside his

big wooden dresser that cool summer

morning by two men in white with a cot

to a Sanitorium over one hundred

miles away

where he ate from a tube, pissed

in a tube, breathed through a tube

and shat upon himself

until he died

the dog and horse still standing proud.

Devil Wind

BY NOAH B. SALAMON

The wind came down the canyon like
a rush of angry blood, like
running soft fingers over an old scar

eddying here in shallow
graves, bent palms tossing
panicked fronds like
startled colts

and blew us out, chasing ash
and flame upon us, until

sun-tired and filthy
exhausted at the coast
it dipped toes in the cold-ruthless
Pacific, and napped

Lament

BY NOAH B. SALAMON

The sun is my only god

back against City Hall's blank white
I can pivot

       to three cardinal points --
the Hall of Justice, Hall of Records

this comic book city
imagining itself real
every day
       out of nothing

like Whitman said
urge and urge and urge --

But I lose myself

Sunburnt and merciless, naked to the waist
I will not lament

my anger
is serene anger

beyond indignation

You! With your insidious
charity smile!

   palms on the simmering sidewalk
resigned, impotent, rage

Lines

BY RHIANNON JAMES-CRESWELL

The two lines that are parallel
Never collide-
Corresponding shapes
Failing   to   unite.

How can identical objects
Congruent, coinciding
Coexist-
Unrelated,
D i s c o n n e c t e d?

Another unavailing anomaly
Contrived by humankind-

An endless cycle With
imaginary lines.

The Question

BY RHIANNON JAMES-CRESWELL

Tirelessly, we wait
Without rhyme or reason,
Codependent on the world's external concepts; Leaving
the soul   detached.

The individual's subjectivity becomes eclipsed Original
abstracts, surrendered.

An intellectual paradox—
The unimaginable, the unattainable
All within the user's grasp.

Biographies

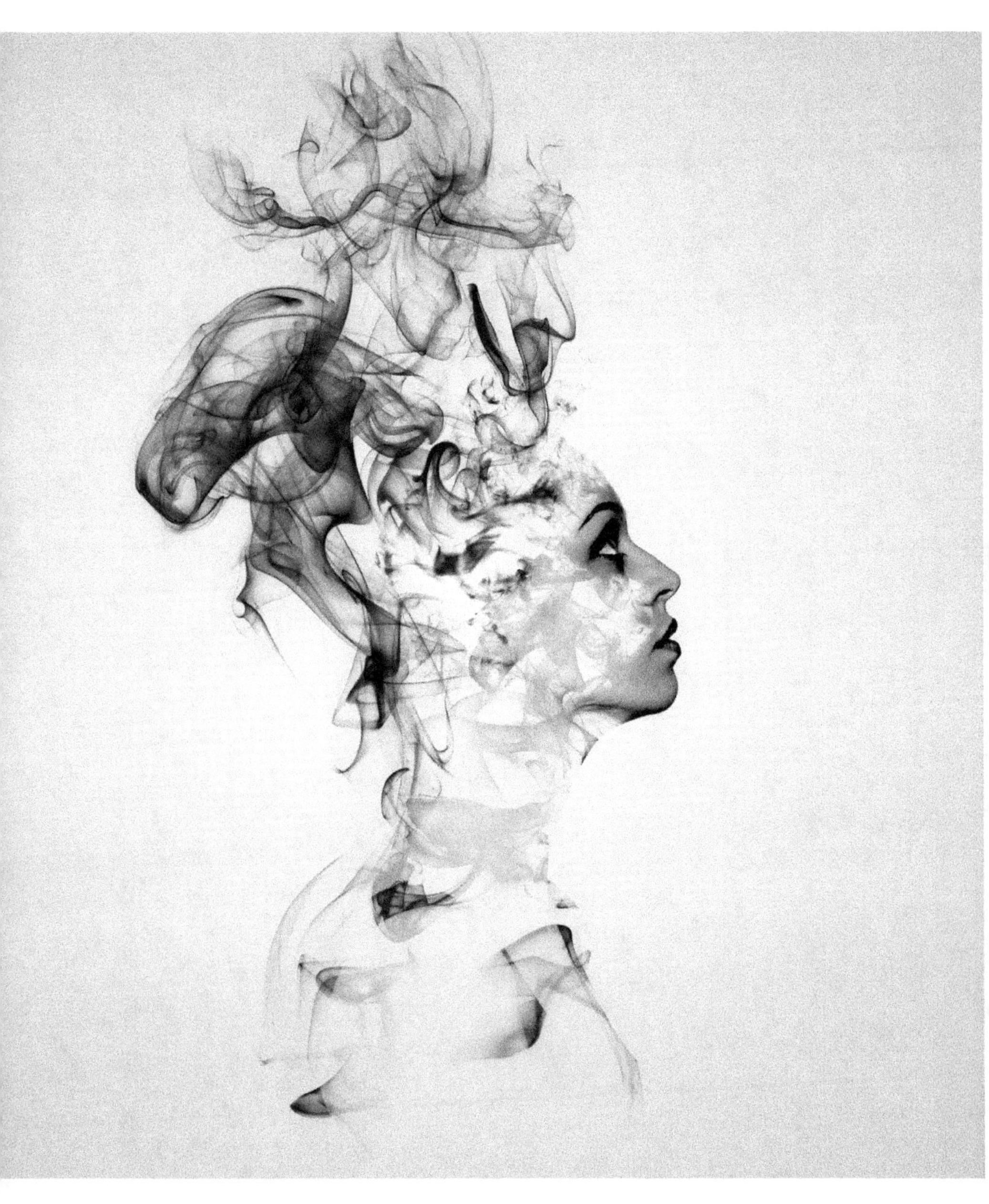

IMAGE BY RICHARD REID (CREATIVECOMMONS.ORG)

Biographies

Prose

P.S. BECKET

P. S. Becket is a freshman English major at the University of Central Oklahoma. He enjoys reading and writing and hopes to become an author someday. He loves books, movies and videogames because of their stories.

RONY KAMPALATH

Rony Kampalath lives in Irvine, CA with his wife, daughter, and dog. His work has previously been published in the Chattahoochee Review.

KATE SPITZMILLER

Kate Spitzmiller's work has appeared in *Approaching Footsteps, On the Premises, Cleaver Magazine, Typishly, The Esthetic Apostle,* and *The Write Launch.* Her flash fiction piece, "Brigida," was nominated for a Pushcart Prize, and her debut novel, Companion of the Ash, was released in December of 2018 by Spider Road Press.

EVAN JAMES SHELDON

Evan James Sheldon's work has appeared in *CHEAP POP, Ghost City Review, Pithead Chapel, Roanoke Review,* and *Typehouse,* among others. He is an Assistant Editor for *F(r)iction* and an Outreach Assistant for Brink Literary Project.

MORGAN SMITH

Morgan Smith is a novelist, playwright, and freshman at Bryn Mawr College, where she is double majoring in Creative Writing and English. Her short stories have been published in the US and the UK, and she reviews upcoming books for Simon and Schuster, Random House, and Harper Collins. She is currently in the process of getting her first book published. Her first musical is in development.

Plays

JACKSON COMPTON

Jackson Compton is a comic book creator, novelist, screenwriter, artist, and filmmaker. Jackson-of-all-trades.

Visual Art

JOSHUA ATLAS

Joshua Atlas grew up in the southwest United States, worked in and out of industrial drafting for years, traveled, extensively as a journeyman and driver. Of late, he increasingly seeks out remote and extreme environments in which to draw—where space is bigger, time moves slower, and perspective is ubiqutous.

RAMONA DARABANT

Ramona Darabant was born in Romania, but now she lives near Vienna, Austria (mountains, no kangaroos). She works as a family physician. In her free time, she writes, paints and chases after the best light and interesting patterns in nature, camera glued to the face.

LIAO DEAN

Liao Dean is an artist living and working in Los Angeles. His works seek to explore contemporary themes and environments by engaging interdisciplinary dialogue and exchange.

ESTEBAN JIMENEZ GUERRA

Esteban Jimenez Guerra was born in La Habana, Cuba in 1984. Currently based in New York. Esteban's work takes a critical look at dominant representations that circulate in popular culture in order to challenge racial and gendered stereotypes. Specifically, Esteban seeks to deconstruct commonly held views of black and female bodies and to offer alternative ways of seeing them. He does this by simultaneously exposing the histories and structures that sustain racism and sexism and by finding provoking ways to reimagine them. In doing this, Esteban draws from the cultural resources of his native Cuba and its rich African heritage as well as from the staggering diversity of New York City, where he currently resides. Often he works on large formats mixing various techniques such as silkscreen, collage, collagraph, and painting. While primarily a painter, he also incorporates photography and sculpture into his work. Overall, he is committed to using art to help us imagine more liberating futures.

JACOB NEWTON

Jacob Newton is a student at the University of Central Oklahoma working on his bachelors in photographic arts. He specializes in fashion photography, but he has also worked on various other forms of photography in the past. His love for photography started when he

was a sophomore in high school while working on the yearbook staff.
He hopes to find himself in a big city one day working with a clothing
company or fashion magazine.

Poetry

ZOË BLAYLOCK
Zoë Blaylock works in healthcare/research ethics at several medical and
academic centers in San Diego. She was formally educated at Harvard.

RAYMOND P. HAMMOND
Raymond P. Hammond is the editor-in-chief of both *The New York
Quarterly* and *NYQ Books*. He holds an MA in English Literature from
New York University and is the author of *Poetic Amusement,* a book
of literary criticism. He lives near Scranton, PA with his wife, the poet
Amanda J. Bradley, and their dog Hank.

ANN HOWELLS
Ann Howells edited *Illya's Honey* literary journal from 1999 to
2017. Her books are *Under a Lone Star* (Village Books) and an
anthology of D/FW poets she edited, *Cattlemen and Cadillacs*
(Dallas Poets Community). Her chapbook, *Softly Beating
Wings,* won the William D. Barney Chapbook Contest for 2017
(Blackbead). She has poems recently published in *Chiron Review,
Slant,* and *Perfume River*, and a collection of Chesapeake Bay
poems were released in the spring (Bowen).

RHIANNON JAMES-CRESWELL
Rhiannon James-Creswell graduated from The University of
Central Oklahoma in 2014 with a BA in English Literature. She
writes poetry as a hobby in her spare time.

NOAH B. SALAMON
Noah B. Salamon is the English Department Chair at Sierra
Canyon School in Chatsworth, California. He received an MA in
English from Loyola Marymount University, where he won the
Graduate Poetry Contest in 2015. His poetry has appeared in *New
Limestone Review, Silver Needle Press, HCE Review* and *Sixfold.*
His essay "The Transformative Effect of Color in the Poetry of
Tomas Tranströmer" was published in the *World Literature Today*
blog in 2014.

SUBMISSION INFORMATION

New Plains Review accepts original work in poetry, prose, and visual art. Submission information and editorial guidelines are accessible through the website.

ORDERING INFORMATION

Pricing for current and back issues are available through Amazon.

UNIVERSITY OF CENTRAL OKLAHOMA
EQUAL OPPORTUNITY STATEMENT

In compliance with Title VI and Title VII of the Civil Rights Act of 1964, Executive Order 11246 as amended, Title IX of The Educaiton Amendments of 1972, Sections 503 and 504 of the Rehabilitation Act of 1973, the Americans with Disabilities Act of 1990, the Family and Medical Leave Act of 1993, the Civil Rights Acts of 1991, and other Federal Laws and Regulations, the University of Central Oklahoma does not discriminate on the basis of race, color, national origin, sex, age, religion, handicap, disability, or status as a veteran in any of its policies, practices or procedures; this includes but is not limited to admissions, employment, financial aid, and educational services.

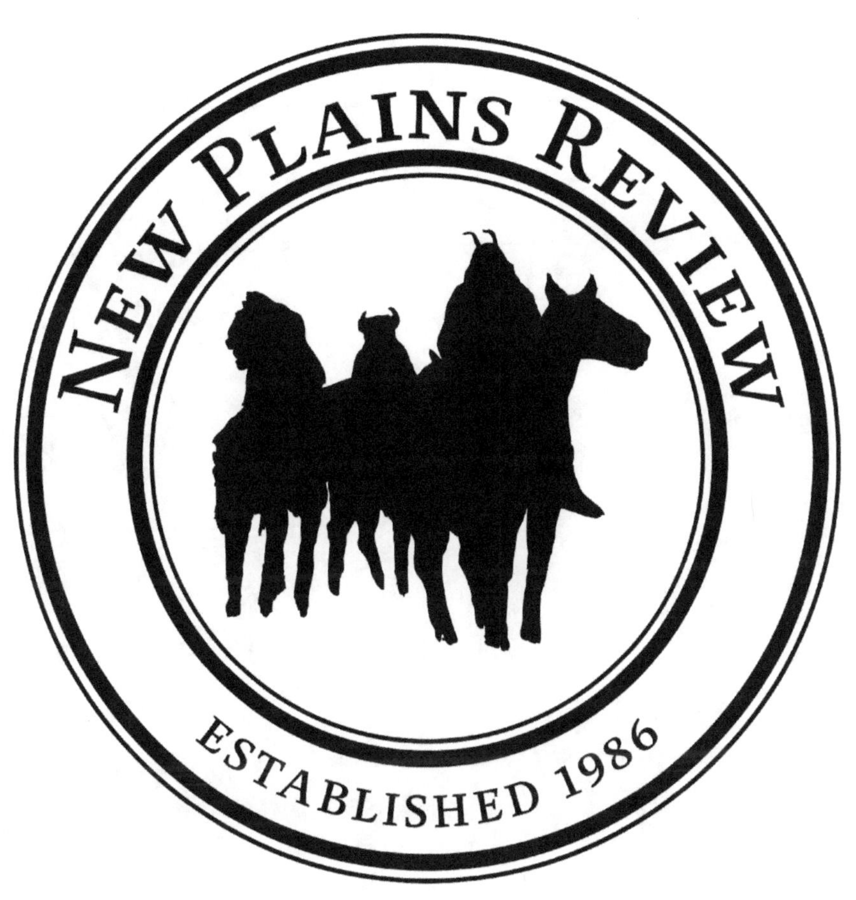

New Plains Review
Established 1986

www.ingramcontent.com/pod-product-compliance
Lightning Source LLC
Chambersburg PA
CBHW061038050726
47592CB00004B/1500